505
BASKETBALL QUESTIONS

YOUR FRIENDS
CAN'T ANSWER

505
BASKETBALL
QUESTIONS

YOUR FRIENDS
CAN'T ANSWER

SOL
BARZMAN

WALKER AND COMPANY ✺ NEW YORK

Library of Congress Cataloging in Publication Data

Barzman, Sol.
  505 basketball questions your friends can't answer.

  1. Basketball—United States—Miscellanea.
I. Title. II. Title: Five hundred and five basketball
questions your friends can't answer.
GV885.7.B36 1981   796.32'3'0973   81-51964
ISBN 0-8027-0690-8   AACR2
ISBN 0-8027-7181-5 (pbk.)

First published in the United States of America in 1981 by the Walker Publishing
Company, Inc.

Published simultaneously in Canada by John Wiley & Sons Canada, Limited,
Rexdale, Ontario

ISBN: 0–8027–0690–8 (cloth)
       0–8027–7181–5 (paperback)

Library of Congress Catalog Card Number: 81-51964

Printed in the United States of America

10 9 8 7 6 5 4 3 2 1

ACKNOWLEDGMENTS

  The author is grateful to the following for their generous help in providing
information: Ed Falk, the National Basketball Association (NBA), New York, New
York; Ellen Sowchek, librarian, National Headquarters of the YMCA, New York,
New York; June Steitz, librarian, the Basketball Hall of Fame, Springfield, Massachusetts; the Public Relations Department, the National Collegiate Athletic Association (NCAA), Shawnee Mission, Kansas; and the Public Relations Department, the Women's Professional Basketball League (WBL), Chicago, Illinois.

Contents

Almost without exception, every major American sport is an adaptation of sports played in other countries or of athletic competitions conducted in ancient times. Even children's games, both imported and native, have contributed to the development of some of our favorite sporting events. "One O' Cat," a children's game still played in some sections of the country, was a primitive variety of baseball; it was being played in New York City and in other parts of the eastern United States long before Abner Doubleday supposedly invented baseball much as we now know it.

Although there is doubt whether Doubleday did in fact invent American baseball, there is no question as to the creation of basketball. It is the only major American sport invented in America, and it is the only American sport that can be clearly dated as to time of creation. We don't know the exact date, but we do know the year. We also know *why* it was created—and who created it.

With that in mind, let's toss the ball in for the center jump, and proceed with the game.

PREGAME WARMUP

The Beginning

1. Who invented basketball?

2. Although he spent most of his adult life in the United States, and died in Lawrence, Kansas, the inventor of basketball was not born in this country. Where was he born?

3. This man devoted his life to teaching, but he had degrees in two other specialties that he never practiced. What were they?

4. Where was basketball invented?

5. When was it invented? Just guess the year, not the actual date.

6. Why was it invented?

7. Where was the first game played?

8. Basketball today is governed by a complex set of rules. How many rules were set up for the first game?

9. We all know that basketball games are played by five players to each side. How many players participated in that first game?

10. Why was this number chosen?

11. In addition to the rules he set up for the first game, the inventor of basketball suggested that the number of players could vary from the number that actually played in the first game. Make an educated guess as to the lowest number he suggested and the highest.

12. In one memorable game played a year or so later, the number of participants resembled a mini-marathon. How many played in that game, and where was it played?

13. What outdoor games influenced the creation of basketball?

14. What is the significance of these dates: December 21, 1891; January 15, 1892; January 20, 1892?

15. What was the original name of basketball?

16. Many amateur basketball teams have sponsors, such as a local hardware store, which will pay for uniforms and other equipment. Who sponsored basketball in its early days?

17. Basketball became an international sport in a relatively short time after its invention What was the reason for its universal popularity?

18. Within three years after its creation, basketball was introduced into two Asian countries. What two countries?

19. Four years later, a third Asian country discovered the game and took it up with great interest. Which country was it? (Hint: This same country now plays baseball with the same enthusiasm.)

20. A few months after the first game of basketball was played, an influential newspaper ran a story about the "new game," sparking enough interest so that basketball began to spread to colleges. What was the newspaper?

21. The inventor of basketball himself played only twice in his entire lifetime—the first time a few weeks after he invented the game, and the second time some seven years later. The second game has little interest for us, but a fellow player in his first game became a legendary college football coach. Who was he?

22. This same player scored the only points for his side. How many goals did he make, and how many goals did the winning side score?

ANSWERS

1. Basketball was invented by Dr. James Naismith, a physical education instructor for the International Young Men's Christian Association. He was thirty years old at the time.

2. Naismith was born in Ontario, Canada. He took his early education at Canada's McGill University and came to the United States in 1890.

3. He was ordained as a Presbyterian minister, but never held a pastorate. He also had an M.D. degree, but never practiced as a physician.

4. Basketball was invented in Springfield, Massachusetts, where Dr. Naismith was teaching for the YMCA Training School. Now known as Springfield College, the school in Naismith's time trained young men to work in YMCAs across the country.

5. Naismith invented the game in the winter of 1891–1892.

6. Dr. Luther S. Gulick, head of the school's physical education department, realized that the young men in his charge did not like the dull routine of dumbbells, parallel bars, marching, and other forms of indoor gymnastics they were required to participate in during the lull between the baseball and football seasons. He assigned Naismith to come up with something more enjoyable. After much deliberation and a number of false tries, Naismith finally hit upon the notion of a game that would require a round ball that could be handled and passed easily from one player to another. He also wanted a high horizontal goal, to emphasize accuracy rather than force, as was the case with the ground-level goals in football and soccer.

7. The first game was played in the gymnasium of the International Young Men's Christian Association Training School in Springfield.

8. *Naismith set up thirteen rules. Many of the principles in those thirteen rules are still embodied in our present-day rules.*

9. *Eighteen players participated in the first game, nine to a side.*

10. *The number was set at nine to a side because that's how many players showed up for that first game.*

11. *In Naismith's own words, "The number composing a team depends largely on the size of the floor space, but it may range from three on a side to forty. The fewer players down to three, the more scientific it may be made, but the more players, the more fun."*

12. *In 1892 Ed Hitchcock, Jr., physical education director at Cornell, heard about Naismith's new game. Because his class contained one hundred students, he divided the class into two teams of fifty each, and threw the first ball up for grabs. The resulting chaos almost brought the gymnasium down, and Hitchcock decided fifty to a side were too many.*

13. *Canadian lacrosse, soccer, and English rugby.*

14. *Although it is generally conceded that the first game of basketball was played in the winter of 1891–1892, not even Dr. Naismith knew the exact date. The three most popular dates suggested are December 21, 1891, January 15, 1892, and January 20, 1892.*

15. *The game was played for some time without a name, until one of the students suggested "Naismith ball." When Naismith objected that no one would ever play a game called "Naismith ball," the same student then suggested "basket-ball." Naismith quickly agreed; eventually the hyphen was dropped for simplification.*

16. *YMCAs.*

17. *The game was carried to the rest of the country, and later to much of the world, by members of various YMCAs, who introduced it in their own gyms.*

18. *Many of the students who attended the International Young Men's Christian Association Training School in Springfield were sent, upon graduation, to foreign countries. In 1894 a YMCA missionary named Bob Gailey introduced the game to Tsientsin,*

China, and in that same year another missionary named Duncan Patton brought the game to India.

19. Japan. The game was brought there by a Japanese graduate of Springfield–Genzabaro Sadakn Ishikawa. Incidentally, Ishikawa made a drawing of the first game for his school newspaper, Triangle, in January 1892.

20. The New York Times ran a story in April 1892 describing "A New Game of Ball." The Times called it "a substitute for football without its rough features."

21. Amos Alonzo Stagg.

22. Stagg scored exactly one goal for his side, which was made up of himself, Naismith, Dr. Gulick, and four other instructors. The winning side, made up of seven YMCA students, scored a total of five goals.

MORE PREGAME WARMUP

The Rules and the Equipment

1. In addition to his set of rules, the inventor of basketball started out with five principles. The first principle seems too obvious to put into writing, and yet he thought it was necessary. What was this first principle?

2. What kind of ball was used in the first game of basketball?

3. Basketballs used today differ slightly in size from the first ball. What are the official dimensions of the basketball now in use?

4. When properly inflated, a basketball must have a particular property. What is it?

5. A man named Stebbins, employed at the institution where basketball was invented, played a most unusual role in the creation of basketball. What role did he play?

6. Stebbins made a further contribution to basektball lore when he was asked to supply an important piece of equipment—it's something you probably have in your garage or toolshed. What was it?

7. What are the dimensions of the basket now in use, and how high must it be above the court?

8. Why was the height set at this distance?

9. The basket we're all familiar with has an open bottom. For some years, however, the baskets were made with closed bottoms. How was the ball retrieved?

10. When was the backboard introduced?

11. Why was it necessary to have backboards?

12. When was it definitely established that the number of players to each team would be five? Give the year.

13. There are certain basic elements of the game we now take for granted, but they weren't part of the original format. The dribble is one of them. Why was the dribble introduced?

14. When did the rules officially recognize the dribble?

15. The inventor of basketball wanted his game to eliminate the roughhouse tactics of football. But one of his rules unfortunately created even more roughhouse and physical contact than football. What was that rule, and how was it modified to our present-day rule, which is far more orderly and much faster? It's a play that occurs often in every game.

16. Present-day official rules stipulate that a college player is disqualified for further play (or fouls out) after five personal fouls; in pro basketball the number of disqualifying fouls is six. What was the number in the original rules?

17. In those same original rules, what was the point value of a field goal and a free throw?

18. How many points were scored in the first game ever played?

19. What are the dimensions of a basketball court?

20. How far is the free-throw line from the basket?

21. A basketball court is divided into sections with three designations. What are these three designations?

22. Pros now play four quarters of 12 minutes each, while colleges play two halves of 20 minutes each. What is the official playing time for (a) high schools, and (b) teams younger than high school age?

ANSWERS

1. In the first of his five fundamental principles, Dr. Naismith specified that "there must be a ball; it should be large, light, and handled with the hands."

2. An "ordinary Association football," or soccer ball. "Association" referred to Young Men's Christian Association.

3. The basketball, always round, must be no less than 29½ inches and no more than 30 inches in circumference. It must weigh between 20 and 22 ounces.

4. When properly inflated, an official basketball should bounce 49 to 54 inches when it is dropped from a height of 6 feet.

5. Mr. Stebbins was the janitor at the Springfield YMCA Training School in 1891–1892, when basketball was invented. Naismith asked him for two boxes, each about 18 inches square, but Stebbins had only peach baskets, about 15 inches in diameter at the top, and tapering to a smaller size at the bottom. Instead of the boxes he originally wanted, Naismith used Stebbins's peach baskets and nailed them to the lower rail of the balcony at each end of the school's gymnasium.

6. Since the peach baskets were closed at the bottom, a way had to be devised to retrieve the ball. Stebbins supplied a ladder for this purpose.

7. The basket must have a rim 18 inches in diameter, with a net of white cord hanging below it for a distance of 15 to 18 inches. The basket must be hung 10 feet above the floor and 4 feet from the end line.

8. The balcony rails in Springfield where Stebbins' peach baskets were nailed were exactly 10 feet high. From that day to this, the height was never changed, despite the many present-

day players who are 6 feet 10 inches, 6 feet 11 inches, and even 7 feet and over. As Naismith himself wrote many years after he first invented the game, "So strong is tradition . . . it is almost heresy to suggest change."

9. *The ball was released by use of a chain and pulley which were attached to the basket. The chain and pulley were operated by the referee, who pulled the handle of the chain to tilt the basket and allow the ball to roll out.*

10. *In 1895. Early backboards were made of a heavy screen, but because there was not enough give for rebounds, they were later changed to wood or "any rigid material," as now specified by the rules.*

11. *To protect the ball from spectators. Before backboards were devised, spectators often sat in the balcony directly behind the basket and helped their own teams by (a) pushing their hands through the balcony rails to shove the ball into the basket for the home team, or (b) batting the ball away for the visitors.*

12. *1897.*

13. *The original 13 rules did not allow the dribble but only permitted the ball to be thrown or batted in any direction with one or both hands. The player could not run with the ball but had to throw it from the spot where he caught it. Under this rule, the player with the ball was frequently hemmed in and helpless when he was too closely guarded to throw the ball. Soon after, it was realized that he could get away from his opponents by bouncing, or dribbling, the ball on the floor. Players were therefore permitted to dribble the ball in any fashion they chose.*

14. *By 1899 the rules were modified to specify that a player could dribble with either hand as often as he had to but could not dribble with both hands more than once. In 1901 another rule stated that a player could not dribble the ball and then shoot for a goal. This was changed in 1908 to the rule now in effect, which states that a player can dribble the ball and then shoot.*

15. *The out-of-bounds play. Originally, Naismith's rules stated that when a ball went out of bounds, the player who first touched it out of bounds was permitted to throw it in without interference. What happened was that almost everyone on both teams went after the out-of-bounds ball with a vengeance; the resulting roughhouse was far worse than football, which at least had some* *semblance of control. Over the years, the out-of-bounds rules were modified until finally, in 1914, the rule was changed to give the ball to the nearest opponent.*

16. Under the original 13 rules, players did not foul out of a game no matter how many fouls they committed. After the first personal foul, a player was warned by the referee; after his second personal foul, the player was disqualified from further play only until the next basket was made, by either side. He then returned to play and repeated the same process over again.

17. One for a field goal. There were no free throws in the early games. Free throws were not permitted until 1894. In 1896 point values were established at two for a field goal and one for a free throw.

18. One. Only one field goal was made during the entire game.

19. Basketball is played on a rectangular court, generally 50 by 94 feet for college and professional teams, 50 by 84 feet for high schools. The rules speak only of "ideal measurements." Since dimensions are not definitely prescribed, some high schools, because of a lack of space, have smaller courts.

20. Fifteen feet.

21. Front court, midcourt, and back court.

22. (a) High schools play four quarters of 8 minutes each, with 10 minutes between halves; (b) teams younger than high school age play four quarters of 6 minutes each, with the same 10 minutes between halves.

PREGAME WARMUP WINDUP

Odds and Ends

1. Terminology in sports frequently overlaps. What six terms in basketball are also to be found in football?

2. One of these terms also applies to golf. Which is it?

3. One other basketball term is used in golf. What is this other term?

4. Billiards has the distinction of being yet a third sport sharing a term with basketball. Name it.

5. One term in basketball applies to a violation, but it means something entirely different in soccer and hockey. What is that term?

6. There is a basketball violation that is perfectly legal in football. What is it?

7. Another basketball violation is also a football violation. Which one?

8. There are two things you can do with a credit card. In basketball these same two things are each a no-no. What are they?

9. Basketball players now use a maneuver you might employ at your breakfast table. Name this showy and crowd-pleasing maneuver.

10. What might you have in your living room that is frequently used during a basketball game?

11. What are two items you might find in your toolshed that are different names for an important piece of equipment in basketball?

12. An important part of the basketball court is something that no home owner or apartment dweller can do without. What is it?

13. Why are basketball players called "cagers"?

14. A defensive maneuver used in basketball might remind you of a heart-to-heart talk between a father and adolescent son. Name this maneuver.

15. A second defensive technique is used both in basketball and football. What is it? (Hint: It is not used by basketball pros.)

16. Basketball has tried some weird variations that never caught on, such as basketball on roller skates. But one basketball variation has successfully survived to much acclaim. Name this variation.

ANSWERS

1. *Pass, time out, out of bounds, turnover, field goal, and conversion. A turnover means that the offensive team loses the ball, or turns it over to the other team. In football, a turnover results from a fumble or an intercepted pass. In basketball, a turnover can be caused by an offensive foul, a violation, the ball going out of bounds, an interception, or a steal. A field goal in football is performed by a kicker, usually a specialist in that one category, and is good for three points. In basketball, a field goal refers to a shot made during play from the court and can court for either two or three points, depending on the length of the shot. A football conversion is a successful one-point kick after a touchdown; a basketball conversion is a successful free throw.*

2. *Out of bounds. In golf, when a golfer hits his ball out of bounds, he loses a stroke. In basketball, when a ball goes out of bounds, it is awarded to a nearby opponent of the player last touching the ball.*

3. *Hook shot. In golf, a hook shot is one that goes to the left of where the golfer intended it; a basketball hook shot is generally made close to the basket and is hooked, with one hand, above the heads of tall defensive players.*

4. *Bank shot, or carom shot.*

5. *Goal-tending. In soccer and hockey, goal-tending, the responsibility of the goalie, is one of the most important parts of the game. In basketball, goal-tending is a violation because it refers to the act of a defending player batting the ball away as it is on a downward path to the basket. If he bats it away on its upward path, it is not a violation. Downward, it is considered a basket, and two points are awarded to the player making the shot.*

6. *Blocking.*

7. *Holding.*

8. *Charging and traveling. If a defensive player has established his position, an offensive player—the one with the ball—is guilty of a foul if he charges into the defensive player. In a traveling violation, the offensive player handling the ball must dribble, or bounce, the ball once for every two steps he takes. If he takes more than two steps without dribbling, he is guilty of traveling, a violation that turns the ball over to the other team.*

9. *Dunking, or jumping high towards the basket and dumping the ball into the basket from above, rather than shooting from the floor.*

10. *A screen. This is a legal method of blocking a defender without making contact. One or more offensive players may set up a screen against a defensive player.*

11. *A bucket or a hoop, other terms for the basket.*

12. *A key, also called the keyhole. This is the free throw lane and free-throw circle. Originally, the free-throw lane was six feet wide a large circle at the top; it actually looked like a keyhole. The lane is now much wider, so that it no longer looks like a keyhole, but it's still called the key or keyhole.*

13. *Early professionals played most of their games on dance floors rather than gymnasiums. Chicken wire was used to keep spectators off the floor, and the players were thus called "cagers."*

14. *Man to man.*

15. *The zone defense.*

16. *Wheelchair basketball. Roller-skate basketball was tried, without success, in 1900 at New York's Madison Square Garden. Promoters tried it at other times over the next few years, but it always failed.*

THE FIRST PERIOD

The Early Pros

1. When was the first professional game played? Don't try to guess the actual date, just the year.

2. Where was it played?

3. Why was it played? This is *not* a catch question. Pros play to earn money, of course, but in the early days there was another reason, perhaps more important.

4. How much did each player earn in that first professional game?

5. It was not until the 1920s that professional basketball players were offered seasonal contracts with a guaranteed salary. Before then, basketball was a wildcat sport with pros jumping back and forth from one team to another or from one league to another. It was not unusual for a pro in the early era to play for a certain team one night, and the following night play on a different team against his teammates of the night before. Players went wherever the money was. How much was the average pay for a night's play in those days?

6. Early pro teams were frequently organized as ethnic groups (although they sometimes used players of other nationalities). One of the most famous of the ethnic teams came out of Buffalo, New York. What was the name of this team?

7. Two other cities later had their own outstanding ethnically named teams. One of these cities was New York.

What was that team called? Watch this one. Part of the name still exists today, but elsewhere.

8. The second team played out of Philadelphia. What was the name of this team?

9. The most famous of all ethnic teams is the Harlem Globetrotters, still going strong today. Although this all-black team was named for a section of New York City, it did not begin there. Where did it start?

10. There was a second great all-black team. This one did play out of New York City. What was its name?

11. Basketball has always delighted in giving its teams exotic names. The early era had its share of unusual names. What city did the "Rosenblums" represent?

12. Here are a few more names to match up with the cities they represented or played out of: (*a*) the Bantams; (*b*) the Blue Diamonds; (*c*) the Jaspers; (*d*) the Palace Five; (*e*) the Roosevelts; (*f*) the Visitations; and (*g*) the Whirlwinds.

13. Early basketball leagues lasted, for the most part, only a season or two. The first, with six teams, called itself the National Basketball League. What year was it organized?

14. Other leagues were organized on a strictly regional basis. In one of these, the Hudson River League of New York state, the dominant team began as an amateur group in Schenectady, New York. When they turned pro, they represented another New York city. What was the name of that city, and what did the team call itself?

15. In 1915 six of the players on this team—including the manager, who also had to function as a substitute player whenever needed—went on a rigorous 39 day barnstorming tour, during which they played 29 games. How many did they win?

16. Their player-manager is in the Basketball Hall of Fame.

His career—as a player, a manager, and a coach—lasted well over 30 years. What is his name?

17. He was responsible for two important basketball innovations. What were they?

18. One feature of basketball you see a lot of now was not possible for the early pros. What was it? And why wasn't it possible?

ANSWERS

1. In 1896.

2. Trenton, New Jersey, in that city's Masonic Hall.

3. Although basketball was being spread throughout the country by various YMCAs, a few "Y's" thought the game too rough and banned it. Forced out of gyms by their local YMCAs, some teams rented dance halls to play in. To pay the rent, they had to charge admission. Anything left over went to the players. This was true for all pro teams during the early years, as well as the Trenton team when it played the first professional game on record.

4. Each player on the Trenton team received $15. Captain · Fred Cooper received $16.

5. In the early wildcat days of basketball, pros received anywhere from $10 to $125 per game, depending upon skill, experience, and crowd appeal. For the "superstars," who appeared in as many as 200 games a season, the pay wasn't bad; the average player, who got the $10, had to struggle to make a living.

6. The Buffalo Germans.

7. The New York Celtics, later called the Original Celtics.

8. The Sphas, or the South Philadelphia Hebrew Association.

9. Chicago.

10. The New York Renaissance, or Rens.

11. Cleveland.

12. (a) The Yonkers Bantams; (b) the Kansas City Blue Diamonds; (c) the Philadelphia Jaspers; (d) the Washington Palace Five; (e) the New York Roosevelts; (f) the Brooklyn Visitations; and (g) the New York Whirlwinds.

13. *1898.*

14. *Troy, New York, Trojans.*

15. *They won all 29 games*

16. *Edward A. Wachter.*

17. *The fast break and the bounce pass. Before then, passing consisted of short tosses caught on the fly by the receivers. The bounce pass, introduced by Wachter's Trojans, was much harder to intercept. In his other innovation, the fast break, he stationed his men in strategic places, with two pursuing the ball, ready to throw it over the defense to an unguarded teammate already set in scoring position. Prior to that, it was the custom for everyone on both teams to scramble after the ball. (In those early days, a center jump was used after every score.)*

18. *The out-of-bounds play. Since the early pros played their games on dance floors—usually 60 by 40 feet—enclosed by chicken wire (later changed to rope), there was no out-of-bounds line anywhere on the floor. Although the chicken wire served to separate the spectators and the players and helped to protect the players from irate fans, it often caused injury to the players. When rope came into use, some players learned how to bounce off the rope and onto an unsuspecting opponent, thus knocking him out of a particular play. We needn't add that this took place before present-day rules were established.*

Time Out: The Ethnic Teams

THE BUFFALO GERMANS

1. As the first famous ethnic team, the Buffalo Germans dominated early professional basketball. Compared to the life span of other pro teams of that era, the Buffalo Germans had a remarkably long life. How many years did they play as a team?

2. They also had one of the most impressive won-lost records ever compiled. How many games did they win, and how many did they lose?

3. They have one other impressive statistic—a tremendous stretch of consecutive victories. How many?

4. In the 1901 Pan-American Exposition held in Buffalo, New York, the Germans won all seven games of the exposition's basketball tournament. The total of their scores *for all seven games* would make a pro team today blush with shame if that's all they scored *in one game*. What was that total?

5. How many points did *all of the losers* score in *all seven games*?

6. By 1905 the Buffalo Germans appeared unbeatable. But in that same year they lost a best two-out-of-three series to a team from Kansas City. The star, and player-manager, of the Kansas City team went on to become one of the greatest of all college basketball coaches. Who was he?

7. In the many years the Buffalo Germans played as a team, they had some outstanding players. How many were elected to the Basketball Hall of Fame?

THE ORIGINAL CELTICS

8. Following the early domination of the Buffalo Germans, the Celtics were probably the best of the pros during the years of their existence. What year were the Celtics organized? Their name at that time was the New York Celtics.

9. When was the name changed to "Original Celtics?" And why was it changed?

10. Another great New York team, the Whirlwinds, had a fine player who later became a legendary New York basketball coach. At the end of the 1921–22 season, an exclusive seasonal contract with a guaranteed salary lured him to the Celtics. Who was this ex-Whirlwind, eventual Original Celtic, and legendary coach?

11. The Celtics had another player who became a legendary New York coach, both in college and professional basketball. Who was he? (Hint: At 6 feet 5 inches, he was one of the first "giants" of the game.)

12. Another player on the Original Celtics (now in the Hall of Fame, as are the two players previously mentioned) accidentally invented one of basketball's most important manuevers. What was it?

13. During the early 1920s a demand that became familiar some years later about another New York team in a different sport was being heard in all of pro basketball. What was it?

14. What was the reason for this demand, and what was its result?

THE SPHAS (THE SOUTH PHILADELPHIA HEBREW ASSOCIATION)

15. The Sphas were the third of the great ethnic teams of the early era. When were they organized?

16. Who organized them?

17. He was originally asked to organize a team for the *North Philadelphia* Young Men's Hebrew Association. But he turned to *South Philadelphia* instead. Why?

18. The organizer of the Sphas had a fascinating nickname. What was it, and why was he given this nickname?

19. The Sphas dominated one of the smaller regional leagues. Which one?

20. After a lapse of four years, the American Basketball League was reorganized for the 1933–34 season. The Sphas switched to the revived ABL and quickly became the top team, easily winning the 1933–34 ABL championship. How many ABL championships did the Sphas win all told?

21. How many *total* championships, including other league play, did the Sphas win?

THE NEW YORK RENS (THE RENAISSANCE)

22. While the original Celtics were overpowering their · white competition, a black team was making a name for itself in New York's Harlem. Who organized that team, and why did he name it the "New York Renaissance"?

23. What year was it organized? How many years did the Rens play together as a team?

24. For the first years of their existence no one bothered to keep track of the Rens' victories or losses. But someone finally started keeping count. How many games did the Rens win after that? How many did they lose?

25. Pro teams today have a roster of twelve players. How many did the Rens have?

26. This number gave rise to a nickname that should remind you of a movie made not too long ago. What was that nickname? (Hint: The movie starred, among others, Yul Brynner and Steve McQueen.)

27. The Rens' center also had a nickname that later became popular in movies and television. Who was he,
and what was his nickname?

28. Are any of the Rens in the Basketball Hall of Fame?

ANSWERS

THE BUFFALO GERMANS

1. *The Germans played together as a team for 30 years, from 1895 to 1925.*

2. *They won 792 games, and lost 86.*

3. *111 straight victories without a loss.*

4. *Eighty-one points for all seven games.*

5. *The losers scored 27 points in all seven games.*

6. *Forrest C. "Phog" Allen.*

7. *None. The team itself, as a unit, was elected to the Basketball Hall of Fame in 1961, but none of the individual players ever made it.*

THE ORIGINAL CELTICS

8. *The Celtics were organized in 1914.*

9. *The name of the team was changed in 1919. The New York Celtics disbanded when the United States entered World War I in 1917. In 1919 two promoter brothers, Jim and Tom Furey, reorganized the Celtics, but the founder of the New York Celtics refused to give up the rights to the name. The Fureys compromised by calling their team the "Original Celtics."*

10. *Nat Holman.*

11. *Joe Lapchick.*

12. *The pivot. It was common at that time for each team to have a standing guard near the foul line. The Celtics used one of their* best shooters, Henry "Dutch" Dehnert, as their standing guard. One night, when the Celtics were playing a team in Miami, Florida, with an insurmountable lead of 30–1, the Celtics decided to practice some of their "set plays," which most other pros were not yet using. But Miami's standing guard kept getting in the way by being stationary and by refusing to move. Dehnert volunteered to stand in front of him with his back to the basket, and whenever the ball was passed to him, he discovered it was a simple matter to turn, or "pivot," away from the other player and go into the basket for a layup.

13. "Break up the Celtics!"

14. The Celtics were beating everyone in sight, playing for the most part as an independent. (They won 90 percent of their games.) When George Preston Marshall, better known as the long-time owner of football's Washington Redskins, organized the American Basketball League in 1926, he forced all of his league's teams to blacklist the Celtics because the Celtics would not join the ABL. With much of their revenue curtailed because of a loss of decent competition, the Celtics relented and joined the American Basketball League midway through the 1926–27 season. Once again the Celtics overwhelmed the opposition, winning 19 of 20 games. The following year they easily won the ABL championship; they were so good that fans began losing interest in the ABL and attendance dropped off drastically. Frustrated rival owners demanded that the Celtics be destroyed as a team. The Celtics were broken up in 1928, and some of their best players were signed by the Cleveland Rosenblums. But whether as Celtics or Rosenblums, these players were still too good. Again they made a shambles of the opposition, and the American Basketball League went out of business.

THE SPHAS (THE SOUTH PHILADELPHIA HEBREW ASSOCIATION)

15. The Sphas were organized in 1918.

16. They were organized by Edward Gottlieb, graduate of the Philadelphia School of Pedagogy. Gottlieb was elected to the Basketball Hall of Fame in 1971.

17. The North Philadelphia Young Men's Hebrew Association never came through with the promised carfare for Gottlieb's team, so he accepted instead the sponsorship of the South Philadelphia Hebrew Association.

18. *Gottlieb's nickname was "The Mogul." He was a super-salesman and promoter. Aside from the Sphas, he organized pro wrestling, Negro baseball, semipro football, and overseas tours for the Harlem Globetrotters. He was one of the early owners in the NBA (the National Basketball Association) and served as chairman of its Rules Committee.*

19. *The Eastern League.*

20. *The Sphas won seven ABL titles in 13 years.*

21. *Eleven.*

THE NEW YORK RENS (THE RENAISSANCE)

22. *The Rens were organized by a St. Kitts native named Bob Douglas. Douglas owned the Renaissance Casino Ballroom, a Harlem nightclub not far from the Cotton Club, the famous Harlem speakeasy owned by racketeer Owney Madden. As competition to the Cotton Club, Douglas organized an all-black basketball team to play in his night club on Sundays and holidays. He named his team after his casino, but because "The Renaissance" was too cumbersome, he shortened it to "The Rens."*

23. *In 1922–23. They played as a team for 25 years.*

24. *Although no one knows for certain how many games the Rens won during their early years, we do have records beginning in 1927. Over the next 21 years, the Rens won 2,318 games and lost 381, for a winning percentage of .859. When the Depression brought ruin to the dance hall business, the Rens were forced to go on the road, where they played for 18 years and appeared in more than 2,000 games.*

25. *They had seven players.*

26. *"The Magnificent Seven."*

27. *Charles "Tarzan" Cooper.*

28. *Yes. Charles "Tarzan" Cooper was inducted into the Basketball Hall of Fame in 1976, when he was tending bar in a rundown neighborhood of South Philadelphia. And the team was inducted as a unit into the Hall of Fame in 1963. Only three other teams have been so honored: "The First Team" (the team that played the very first game) in 1959; the Original Celtics, also in 1959; and the Buffalo Germans in 1961. In 1971 Bob Douglas, owner of the Rens, was elected to the Basketball Hall of Fame as a "Contributor."*

THE HARLEM GLOBETROTTERS

1. They are the most successful basketball team ever assembled, although strictly speaking they are no longer a team playing basketball, but rather a show business attraction specializing in basketball comedy, and they are not one team, but several. In the beginning, however, the Harlem Globetrotters were organized just to play basketball and to try, legitimately, to beat all opponents, which they usually did. Who organized them?

2. Why did he call them "The Harlem Globetrotters"?

3. When did they play together for the first time as a team? And where?

4. Success did not come quickly to the Globetrotters. One night, they played before a handful of people and came away with a total of two dollars and forty cents. But they persisted and found some measure of fame when they began to develop their comedy routines. Aside from the laughs that started them on the road to worldwide renown, the Globetrotters had another reason for perfecting their dazzling displays of ballhandling. What was it?

5. It wasn't until 1940 that the Globetrotters finally hit the big time with a spectacular feat. What was it?

6. Later that year one of their most famous players, "Goose" Tatum, joined the team. What was Tatum's first name?

7. How did he acquire his famous nickname?

8. When the Globetrotters signed him, he had never played basketball seriously, but was a star in another sport. Which sport?

9. Tatum was drafted into the armed services during World War II. To replace him while he was away, the Globetrotters hired a most unusual ballhandler named Bob Karstens. What was so different about him?

10. Karstens played as a Globetrotter during the 1942 season and half of 1943. After that, although he did not wear a Globetrotter uniform, he had a very important role in the Globetrotter organization. What did he do?

11. By 1947 the Globetrotters had become an international team. And they had acquired Nat Clifton, another of their legendary shotmakers and sleight-of-hand magicians. Like Tatum, he too had a nickname that has taken its place in basketball lore. What was it, and how did he get that name?

12. He made another kind of basketball history in 1950. What did he do?

13. In the late 1940s the Harlem Globetrotters were not only the funniest basketball team in the world, but, in a game played without their usual antics, proved they were also the best by beating the most powerful all-white pro team of its day. What team?

14. In the 1950s the Globetrotters began the first of a long string of international travels that have, since then, taken them to almost every country in the world. One year they played before the largest crowd ever to witness a basketball game. How many attended that game, and where was it played?

15. The following year they did their famous warm-up routine, including their popular warm-up song, before the *smallest* crowd ever to watch them. How large was that crowd, and what was the occasion?

16. A third legendary funnyman-shotmaker, their new "Clown Prince" of basketball, joined the team in December of 1954. Who was he?

17. Four years later a man who singlehandedly revolutionized pro basketball played with the Globetrotters for one season before joining the NBA. Who was he?

18. The Globetrotters claim they have one mind-boggling

stretch of "wins" that includes 2,495 "victories" without a loss. That unbelievable win streak was finally broken on January 5, 1971. Who beat them, and where?

19. The man who engineered that defeat has one other basketball distinction. What is it?

20. On the evening of December 6, 1974, the Globetrotters celebrated an event that may never be equaled. What was it?

21. Who are the Washington Generals, the New York Nationals, the New Jersey Reds, the Boston Shamrocks, the Atlantic City Sea Gulls, and the Chicago Demons?

22. The Globetrotters have their own peculiar language. What do they call their famous razzle-dazzle routines?

ANSWERS

1. The Harlem Globetrotters were organized by Abraham Michael Saperstein, more familiarly known as Abe. He was the English-born son of Polish immigrants who moved to Chicago when Abe was a child.

2. Three members of the "Savoy Big Five," an all-black basketball team organized to play in the Chicago branch of New York's famous Savoy Ballroom, quit that group and decided to organize their own team. They asked Abe Saperstein, who was then coaching an all-black basketball team sponsored by an American Legion post, to be their manager-coach. At five feet three inches, Abe Saperstein had a small physique, but huge dreams. He called the new group "Saperstein's Harlem, New York, Globetrotters" (an unwieldy name he later simplified to the "Harlem Globetrotters"). He chose Harlem to show that his team was black, and Globetrotters for the international flavor he confidently expected they would one day have.

3. The team was organized in the winter of 1926 and played its first game on January 7, 1927, in Hinckley, Illinois, a small town some fifty miles west of Chicago.

4. The Globetrotters had a backbreaking schedule that saw them play almost every day, and sometimes two or more games on a single day, and they frequently had to sleep in their Model-T Ford because hotels would not accommodate blacks. Aside from the laughs their ballhandling routines were starting to get, they realized that the dazzling passing of the ball back and forth, almost faster than the eye could see, gave the illusion of continuous movement, when actually their legs and most of their bodies were standing still, thus giving them a much needed rest from the rigors of their continuous barnstorming.

5. *In March 1940 the Globetrotters won the World Championship of Professional Basketball by defeating George Halas' Chicago Bruins 31–29 in the final game of the tournament. In the quarter-finals the Globetrotters had defeated the defending champs, the New York Rens, by a score of 37–36.*

6. *Tatum's first name was Reece.*

7. *At 6 feet 3 inches, Tatum had arms that hung down to his knees. He had an incredible reach of 84 inches. During a high-school football game he jumped high into the air for a pass and reached out with his arms in what seemed like an impossible stretch. Someone in the stands yelled, "Look at the ol' Goose fly!" The nickname stuck with him for the rest of his life.*

8. *Baseball. He played left field for the Birmingham Black Barons of the Negro Baseball League.*

9. *Karstens was white, the only white man, aside from Abe Saperstein himself, ever to play for the Globetrotters.*

10. *After Tatum returned, Karstens was released, and he organized a permanent opposition team to play against the Globetrotters. Karstens called his team the Boston Whirlwinds.*

11. *Clifton's nickname was "Sweetwater"—a name given to him in high school because of his addiction to soda pop.*

12. *Nat "Sweetwater" Clifton and Charles "Chuck" Cooper were the first black players to compete in the NBA. In 1950 Clifton was signed by the New York Knicks and Cooper was signed by the Boston Celtics. Although Clifton did not set any records, in eight seasons of NBA ball he scored the respectable total of 5,444 points.*

13. *In February 1948, before 17,000 fans in Chicago Stadium, the Harlem Globetrotters defeated the Minneapolis Lakers in one of the most exciting games ever played. The final score was 61–59, with the Globetrotters scoring the winning basket just as the gun went off. Among others, the Lakers had on their team two of the greatest players of all time—George Mikan and Jim Pollard.*

14. *Seventy-five thousand, in the Olympic Stadium, Berlin, Germany.*

15. *During a tour through Europe in 1952 the Globetrotters* were granted an audience by Pope Pius XII. With the Pope as a crowd of one, five of the Globetrotters performed their famous warm-up routine, while Abe Saperstein and the rest of the team provided the musical accompaniment, clapping and whistling "Sweet Georgia Brown." The Pope's feet could be seen tapping along beneath his flowing garments.

16. Meadowlark Lemon.

17. Wilt Chamberlain.

18. On January 5, 1971, in Martin, Tennessee, the Globetrotters were defeated for the first time in 2,496 games. The team that beat them was their current traveling opposition, owned by a white player named Herman "Red" Klotz. In the last minute of play Klotz made three long two-hand set shots—his specialty—and his opposition team, much to the shock of the Globetrotters, won the game, 100–99.

19. At 5 feet 7 inches, Klotz was the smallest man ever to play in the NBA. He played eleven games for the Baltimore Bullets during the 1947–48 season, when the Bullets won the NBA championship.

20. They played their 12,000 game on December 6, 1974.

21. They are all different names for the Globetrotters' permanent traveling opposition team.

22. Reems.

Second Time Out: More Odds and Ends

While the opposing coaches settle their players down or try to regroup during this second time out, let's take our own breather with a few anecdotes from the early and middle years of basketball.

When James Naismith first came to the YMCA Training School in Springfield, Massachusetts, he participated in contact sports with a peculiarly refined zest. He once preached a sermon at Springfield while sporting two black eyes from a football game. He was, in the words of one basketball historian, "the jock-minister personified." The captain-coach of the YMCA Springfield football team, Amos Alonzo Stagg, assigned the 160-pound Naismith to play center for the Springfield eleven, affectionately known as "Stagg's Stubby Christians." When Naismith asked why Stagg had chosen him for this position, Stagg answered, "Jim, I play you at center because you can do the meanest things in the most gentlemanly manner."

Although the Buffalo Germans won most of their games with relative ease, one game in 1901 must surely rank among the more memorable. In the seventh and final game of the Pan-American Exposition in Buffalo, New York, the Germans were playing St. Joseph's of Paterson, New Jersey. Three of the Germans were late, and they had only three men left to start the game. For seven minutes these three valiantly kept the St. Joseph's five to a 1–1 tie. At that point one of the tardy Germans furiously pedaled up on his bicycle, and two minutes later a fifth German raced onto the court, but he had to play the rest of the first half in his street clothes. The Buffalo Germans eventually won the game 10–1.

John "Honey" Russell, one of the most durable of the early pros—he played more than 3,200 games with such teams as the Chicago Bruins, Rochester Centrals, and Brooklyn Visitations—vividly recalled some of the wild trips his teams made to Springfield, which had a pro team in the Massachusetts League:

"Every time we played in Springfield I wound up playing against Snooks Dowd. Snooks was a colorful guy in every game he played—basketball, football, or baseball. . . . Snooks was a cute one. He would maneuver me to the side on which his mother was sitting, right against the net and she'd jab me with her hatpin every chance she got."

Conditions were sometimes just as painful for the Original Celtics. They frequently played in "enemy territory," and had to endure various indignities inflicted upon them by the fans. One of the places they dreaded the most was a dance hall in South Brooklyn, New York, where so many fans were jammed in, it seemed "they were hanging from the rafters." These fans thought nothing of flinging a bottle at a Celtic when he was trying to shoot a foul. Or tripping a Celtic rushing down the court. Or jabbing a lighted cigarette into the back of a Celtic's legs. These fans were, as one Celtic characterized them, "holy terrors." No wonder that this particular dance hall, officially known as Prospect Hall, was called by the Celtics "The Bucket of Blood."

The Sphas, the South Philadelphia Hebrew Association, encountered their own share of violence, but they turned at least some of this violence to their advantage. Their home games, always played on a Saturday night at Philadelphia's Broadwood Hotel, were immensely popular, for they were inevitably preceded by a fistfight. As their organizer, Edward Gottlieb, later told the story, "The Sphas used to guarantee a fight every game. Joe Sheehan and our Chickie Passon would start fighting right after they shook hands." And right after the game, Gil Fitch, a former player from Temple then starring for the Sphas, would change into a tuxedo and lead a dance band for the dance that followed every Saturday night game. For these three stellar attractions—fistfight, basketball game, and dance—the fans paid thirty-five cents.

The unique wizardry that has become the Harlem Globetrotters' hallmark, their fast and furious ballhandling, their constant chatter, their comedy routines, did not spring into full bloom overnight. It took years of experimentation, of constant practice, to bring them to their present point of comic mastery on a basketball court. But in a sense, it began accidentally one winter night many years ago, not too long after they first came together as a team.

The Globetrotters were playing on that frigid night in Williamsburg, Ohio, against a local team, in an old meeting hall. Because of the extreme cold, pot-bellied stoves at both ends of the hall were red hot. During the action beneath one of the baskets, a Globetrotter named William "Kid" Oliver backed into a pot-bellied stove. He let out a shriek of anguish, and took off like a skyrocket, trailing smoke behind him. The crowd loved it; they thought it was an act.

For the Globetrotters, the laughter was inspiration enough. From that point on they began inserting little pieces of business into their ball-handling. So it can be said that Kid Oliver scorched his posterior for posterity.

After Jackie Robinson shattered the color barrier in sports in 1947 by breaking into major league baseball with the Brooklyn Dodgers (now the Los Angeles Dodgers), pro basketball flirted with the notion of breaking its own color line. The American Basketball League, which later became the Eastern League, met in Philadelphia in 1947 to discuss admitting the New York Rens to their all-white league. The white owners said no.

When Bob Douglas, owner of the Rens, heard the news,

he was shattered. Douglas always behaved with the greatest dignity, and insisted that his Rens do the same. He did not approve of the Harlem Globetrotters displaying themselves as cheerful, comic minstrels, even though these antics made Abe Saperstein a millionaire. A few months before he died in 1979, Douglas said, "When I go, it will be without a dime in my pocket, but a clear conscience. I could never have burlesqued basketball. I loved it too much for that."

The Harlem Globetrotters have never thought of themselves as "comic minstrels." They take themselves and their game as seriously as did the Rens. They have become America's unofficial "good-will ambassadors," for they have broken through many cultural and communications barriers. One game they played in 1951 aptly demonstrated their accomplishments. *True* magazine described that event:

"August 22, 1951. The largest crowd ever to see a basketball game anywhere in the world—75,000 Germans— gathered in Berlin's Olympic Stadium, scene of many a Hitler rant against 'inferior' people of the world, and went wild over a Black basketball team that was owned by a Jew—one of the crowning ironies in history."

To add to the drama, an Army helicopter landed on the field during half-time with Jesse Owens, the great black track star who had electrified the world with four gold medals in the 1936 Berlin Olympics. In 1936, Owens' victories were met with stony silence from the huge stands, and Hitler angrily stalked from the stadium. Now, however, in 1951, as Jesse Owens hopped out of the helicopter, he was hailed with a thundering ovation that lasted over five minutes. And the mayor of West Berlin greeted him with these words:

"Fifteen years ago on this field Hitler refused to offer you his hand. Now I give you both of mine."

THE SECOND PERIOD

Colleges—The Early Years: From Point a Game to Point a Minute

1. Within two or three years after basketball was invented it began to spread to colleges. What was the first college to play a full basketball schedule?

2. On February 9, 1895, the first basketball game between *two colleges* took place. Which two colleges? Who won that game, and what was the score?

3. When was the first intercollegiate game with *five men on a team* played?

4. Who participated in that game? And who won, by what score?

5. Fourteen months later two eastern teams played the first intercollegiate game in that region with five men per team. What two schools? Which team won, by what score?

6. Basketball was not limited to men. Women played it just as enthusiastically. A few weeks after the very first game was played, a team of local Springfield, Massachusetts girls played against a team of women teachers. One of the young women in that game made another kind of contribution to basketball history. Who was she, and what did she do?

7. What year was *intersectional* basketball introduced?

8. What eastern team introduced intersectional competition?

9. The following year this same team won the championship of the first collegiate basketball league ever organized. What was the name of that league?

10. What were the five teams that made up this league?

11. For its first 15 or so years collegiate basketball was dominated by eastern teams. By 1908, however, domination began to shift to the Midwest. One small midwestern college claimed "the world championship" for a stretch of four years, from 1908 through 1911. What college?

12. How many games did it win during that four year period, and how many did it lose?

13. A few years later, beginning in December 1919, another organization had a succession of "Wonder Teams" that had a staggering stretch of victories without a loss. What was this organization? It was not a college, nor was it a pro team. (Hint: Try Passaic, New Jersey.)

14. How many consecutive games did these "Wonder Teams" win?

15. During the first three or four decades of collegiate basketball, fan interest remained more or less regional, except for a few outstanding teams. One state university in the East compiled a 43–3 record in the 1920 and 1921 seasons. Which university?

16. In 1922 and 1923 a midwestern state university won 33 and lost 3. Name this university.

17. In the Far West the Pacific Coast Conference title was won four times in a row, between 1924 and 1927, by the same university. Which one?

18. Back in the East, a team that came to be known as the "Wonder Five" compiled an impressive record of 86

victories against 8 defeats over a four year period beginning in 1927. Name this team.

19. After graduation the same "Wonder Five" moved as a
unit into the pro ranks and played for many years in the
American Basketball League. As pros, their teams had
two names. What were they?

20. A major three-team rivalry that still continues today
began in the 1920s. What are these three schools? They
are all in the same midwestern state.

21. The old-style, low scoring games went the way of the
peach basket with the development of a fast-breaking
style of play during the early 1930s. Basketball had at
last reached what many considered to be the
ultimate—"a point a minute." What eastern college is
generally credited with developing this free-wheeling,
point-a-minute type of play?

ANSWERS

1. The University of Chicago, with a schedule of seven games, winning six. Coached by Amos Alonzo Stagg, Chicago played its first game in 1894, against the Chicago YMCA Training School, and won by a score of 19–11.

2. Minnesota State School of Agriculture and Hamline College. Minnesota won that first intercollegiate game, 9–3.

3. January 16, 1896.

4. University of Chicago and University of Iowa in Iowa City, Iowa. Chicago won that game, 15–12.

5. The first eastern intercollegiate game with five men on each team was played on March 20, 1897, by Yale and Pennsylvania. Yale defeated Pennsylvania quite handily, by a score of 32–10. For some years Yale was the nation's top collegiate basketball team.

6. One of the young women who played in that first women's game in March 1892 was named Maude Sherman. She married Dr. James Naismith, the inventor of basketball.

7. 1900.

8. Yale.

9. The Eastern League, which later became the Ivy League.

10. Columbia, Cornell, Harvard, Princeton, and Yale.

11. Wabash College of Indiana.

12. Wabash won 66 games, while losing 3.

13. The "Wonder Teams" represented Passaic High School of Passaic, New Jersey.

14. Beginning with a win over Newark Junior College on December 17, 1919, and stretching through February 6, 1925, when Passaic finally lost to Hackensack High by a score of 39–35 the "Wonder Teams" piled up an amazing record of 159 straight victories.

15. Pennsylvania.

16. Kansas.

17. California.

18. St. John's University of New York.

19. The Brooklyn Jewels and the New York Jewels.

20. Indiana, Purdue, and Notre Dame.

21. University of Rhode Island.

Time out: The Early Coaches and All-Stars

All of the players and coaches in the following section are members of the Basketball Hall of Fame.

1. At a time when scores of 9–8 and lower were commonplace, one college player, Christian Steinmetz, had a fantastic scoring spree in 1905. In one game he scored *50 points*. What university did he attend?

2. In addition to being the first player to score 50 points in one game, Steinmetz established two other records that stood for many years. Name them.

3. He was elected to the Basketball Hall of Fame in 1961, but he had another honor bestowed upon him by his home state. What was it?

4. Amos Alonzo Stagg is probably better known as a football coach, but he had a distinguished career as a basketball coach as well at the University of Chicago, where he coached both sports, and much later, at the College of the Pacific. But he is responsible for another achievement that few people associate with him, yet in itself is known to sports fans everywhere. What did he do?

5. One of Chicago's first star players, John J. Schommer, achieved a record any college player would be happy to have. What did he do?

6. Another Hall of Famer was only 5 feet 4 inches, considered too small for high school basketball. But he wasn't too small to become the leading scorer for the City College of New York for three straight years and serve as captain of CCNY's basketball team in 1910. After graduation from CCNY he had a long career as one of the great early pros, and later as a coach. Name him.

7. Hall of Famer John S. Roosma played on one of Passaic High School's "Wonder Teams." The coach of those teams called him "Passaic's Greatest." But he achieved greater basketball renown as a college player. He earned 10 letters, and led his team to 73 wins and 13 losses. What school did he attend? You'll find it in the Northeast.

8. Hall of Famer Paul Endacott starred for one of the great *midwestern* teams of the 1920s. Name his school.

9. In 1923 he won the top honor for collegiate basketball players. What honor?

10. In that same year he helped his team win its own supreme honor. What was it?

11. Only one man has been elected to the Basketball Hall of Fame *twice*, the first time as a player, and the second time as a coach. Name him. He played his collegiate basketball at Purdue University.

12. Another Hall of Fame coach, H. Clifford Carlson, won national championships in 1928 and 1930. What school did he coach?

13. In 1931–32 he made a bold move with his team that had far-reaching results. What did he do?

14. Notre Dame, during the first decades of the twentieth century, was a household name because of its football prowess. But its basketball teams, if not as well known, compiled their own impressive records. Who was their coach?

15. He coached Notre Dame basketball for a 20-year span. How many games did he win, and how many did he lose?

16. He gave up another profession to concentrate on basketball. What profession?

17. Who was the coach responsible for the University of Rhode Island's fast-break high-scoring "point a minute"?

ANSWERS

1. *University of Wisconsin.*

2. *He averaged 25.7 points per game in 1905, and he was the first college player to score over 1,000 points.*

3. *He was selected as one of Wisconsin's All-time Athletic Greats.*

4. *Amos Alonzo Stagg organized the Big Ten Conference.*

5. *Schommer led Big Ten scoring in three straight years— 1907, 1908, and 1909. He was also the first University of Chicago athlete to win 12 letters.*

6. *Barney Sedran.*

7. *West Point. Roosma served in the Army from 1926 through 1956, and retired with the rank of Colonel.*

8. *Paul Endacott attended the University of Kansas.*

9. *He was selected by the Helms Foundation as national Player-of-the-Year in 1923.*

10. *The Kansas Jayhawks won the mythical national championship in 1923. They had the first-ever undefeated record in conference play.*

11. *John R. Wooden.*

12. *H. Clifford Carlson coached Pittsburgh for 31 years.*

13. *He was the first basketball coach to take an eastern team to the West Coast, in 1931–32.*

14. *George E. Keogan.*

15. His Notre Dame teams won 327 games and lost 96, for an impressive .773 percentage.

16. He studied dentistry, but gave it up for basketball.

17. Frank W. Keaney. Speed was always his forte. As a college athlete, he played four sports, including baseball. In 1910 he stole 38 bases, a college record.

Play Resumes: The College Tournaments

The modern era in basketball began during the early 1930s. On December 29, 1934, 16,188 fans crowded into New York's Madison Square Garden to watch a basketball doubleheader promoted by a New York sportswriter. (This was at the old Madison Square Garden on Eighth Avenue at Forty-ninth and Fiftieth streets.)

This first doubleheader at the Garden was follwed by seven more. These eight programs of basketball drew 99,955 people, an average of more than 12,000 for each—a tremendous gate during the Depression years. Over the first six years of college basketball at the Garden, attendance totalled 1,014,000.

The growing popularity of college basketball led to the start of the National Invitational Tournament (NIT) to be staged at the Garden at the end of every season. And that in turn led to the National Collegiate Athletic Association (NCAA) tournament.

The NCAA tournament today, while still invitational in character, consists only of conference champions and major independents. For its first several years, however, the NCAA invited teams other than conference champions or major independents. The NCAA is played in a different college gymnasium each year, rather than in one established location, as is the NIT at the Garden.

1. Who was the sportswriter responsible for promoting the Madison Square Garden doubleheaders?

2. The story has persisted (and never been denied) that a torn piece of clothing owned by this sportswriter inspired him to promote the phenomenally successful basketball doubleheaders at the Garden. What piece of clothing? And what did it have to do with modern basketball?

3. Which four colleges participated in the first Garden doubleheader of December 29, 1934?

4. Who won the opener? By what score?

5. Who won the nightcap? By what score?

6. One of the powerhouse college teams of the 1930s was Long Island University. Who was their coach? He was a popular writer of sports books for young adults as well as a famous basketball coach.

7. Almost two years to the day after the first doubleheader at the Garden, LIU was scheduled to meet a West Coast team in the second half of another doubleheader at the Garden. Up to that evening LIU had a fantastic stretch of consecutive wins. How many?

8. On that memorable evening, December 30, 1936, the largest crowd of the year, 17,623 wildly enthusiastic fans, jammed into the Garden. They had come to cheer two local teams, New York University, playing the first half of the doubleheader, and Long Island University in the second half. NYU lost the opening game. Who beat them, by what score?

9. In the second half of the doubleheader, LIU's streak of consecutive wins finally came to an end; LIU was decisively beaten by the Western team, champions of the Pacific Coast Conference. Name that team, and give the score.

10. One of the most widely publicized superstars of the 1930s was a player from the West Coast team. Who was he?

11. He stunned not only the LIU team, but the Garden fans and New York sportswriters as well, with a maneuver that he had developed which was to bring a new dimension to basketball. What was it?

12. By 1938 college basketball had become a nationwide attraction. In that same year, the Metropolitan Basketball Writers Association of New York organized the first ever major postseason tournament, the National Invitational (NIT). Six teams were invited. Name the two finalists, and name the team that won that first NIT.

13. The following year the National Collegiate Athletic Association organized its own postseason tournament, the NCAA. Where was it played, and who won that first NCAA championship?

14. Name the first team to win *two NIT* titles, and give the years.

15. Name the first team to win *two NCAA* titles, and give the years.

16. A number of teams have won two NIT titles, and two teams have won three. But only one team has won *four* NIT championships. What team?

17. Who was their coach?

18. In 1950 City College of New York accomplished something that had never been done before. What was it?

19. This same feat can never be accomplished again. Why not?

20. Who was CCNY's coach?

21. CCNY's unusual accomplishment of 1950 involved another school—the number-one team in the country. Name it.

ANSWERS

1. Edward "Ned" Irish, sportswriter for the New York World Telegram.

2. Ned Irish was assigned one night to cover a game that was to take place in the small, cramped gymnasium of New York's Manhattan College. By the time he got there the gym was crowded, and the only way Irish could get in was to climb through a window. He tore his pants, and decided on the spot that there had to be a better way to accommodate basketball fans, who jammed into college gyms holding perhaps 1,000 people. He made a deal with Madison Square Garden to present intersectional doubleheaders at the Garden. He quit his job as a sportswriter to devote himself full time to his doubleheaders, the first of which took place on December 29, 1934, to a success even greater than he had anticipated. Irish later helped to organize the NBA, and he formed the New York Knicks in 1946. Ned Irish was elected to the Hall of Fame in 1964. No one knows what happened to his torn pants, which helped to start it all.

3. Westminster, St. John's, New York University, and Notre Dame.

4. In the leadoff game Westminster beat St. John's, by a score of 37–33.

5. The nightcap was not quite as close. NYU beat Notre Dame 25–18.

6. Clair Bee.

7. Forty-three.

8. In the first half of that famous doubleheader, Georgetown defeated NYU, 46–40.

9. *In the nightcap, the game that most of the 17,623 fans had come to see, the Pacific Coast champs, Stanford University, overwhelmed the New York area favorites, by a score of 45–31.*

10. *Angelo "Hank" Luisetti.*

11. *Luisetti had perfected a one-handed jump shot that not only stunned his LIU opponents, the New York fans, and the New York sportswriters but revolutionized basketball as well. Up to then the standard way to shoot was with a two-handed set shot. The one-handed jump shot added excitement and speed to the sport. In his memorable Garden debut of December 30, 1936, Luisetti scored 15 of his team's 45 points.*

12. *Temple and Colorado. The winner was Temple, 60–36.*

13. *The finalists in the first NCAA tournament were the University of Oregon and Ohio State. The game was played at Northwestern's Patten Gymnasium in Evanston, Illinois. Oregon was the winner, 46–33.*

14. *Long Island University, under coach Clair Bee, in 1939 and 1941.*

15. *Oklahoma A. & M., 1945 and 1946.*

16. *St. John's—in 1943, 1944, 1959, and 1965. Bradley was the other team to win three NIT titles—in 1957, 1960, and 1964.*

17. *Joe Lapchick.*

18. *City College of New York won both the NIT and the NCAA championships in the same year 1950 For CCNY this was the "grand slam" of basketball.*

19. *The rules were changed to prohibit college teams from appearing both in the NIT and the NCAA in the same year.*

20. *Nat Holman.*

21. *The number-one team in the country in 1950 was Bradley, which faced CCNY in the finals of both the NIT and the NCAA. Bradley lost both games to CCNY—the NIT by a score of 69–61, and the NCAA, 71–68. Both games were played that year at Madison Square Garden.*

Second Time Out: Still More Odds and Ends

1. Name these three early basketball participants who were better known for their accomplishments in other fields: (a) from Carlisle, he excelled in football and track, and is considered the greatest all-around athlete of his time; (b) from Bucknell, he is one of baseball's all-time great pitchers, with 373 victories against 188 losses, 1901–1916; and (c) from West Point, he was one of the most famous generals in World War II, as commander of U.S. forces in the China-Burma-India area.

2. This basketball star from Colorado, a household name in the 1930s because of his exploits on the football field, had a big season on the basketball court in 1937–38. He later went to England as a Rhodes scholar, and today is one of the more prominent men in Washington, D.C. Who is he?

3. Hank Luisetti, who made such an auspicious debut in New York in 1936, lost a year of eligibility after the end of the 1938 season. Why?

4. Admittedly one of the genuine superstars of his time, Luisetti never went on to play pro basketball. Again why?

5. One prominent New York coach (now in the Hall of Fame) scoffed at Luisetti's one-handed jump shot. Who was he, and what did he say about the one-handed shot?

6. Two rule changes in 1937 brought even more excitement for basketball fans and led to a much faster style of play. Name them.

7. The University of Oregon basketball players were officially known as the Webfeet. But because of three tall men on their NCAA championship team of 1939—two were 6 feet 4 inches and one was 6 feet 9 inches, unusually tall for that time—they were given another nickname, far more picturesque and more appropriate to their home state. What was that nickname?

8. This captain of the University of Illinois basketball team was suspended in 1938 because he allegedly received monthly payments from the Cleveland baseball club of the American League. After he left Illinois, he made a name for himself in major league baseball as a player for the same Cleveland Indians, and later as a manager. Who was he?

9. Another all-around college athlete named Chip Hilton set many records, yet you won't find him listed in any NCAA record books. Why not?

10. Two players of the 1940s did find their way into the record books and into the Basketball Hall of Fame. Both were midwestern giants, apparently awkward, but agile enough to dominate college and pro basketball during their time. One of these stars was 6-foot 10-inch George Mikan. Name the school he attended. It is still a basketball power today.

11. Mikan had originally planned to enter another field of endeavor, but gave it up because of a "deficiency in Greek and an efficiency in basketball." What was it he gave up for basketball?

12. Who was his college coach?

13. Mikan's rival for dominance in the college ranks of the 1940s was an even bigger giant—7-foot Bob Kurland.

What school did Kurland attend? You should know this one. Kurland helped his school win two consecutive NCAA titles.

14. Who was Kurland's college coach? He's another of the legendary college coaches now in the basketball Hall of Fame.

15. Although not very fast, Kurland was remarkably well coordinated for a seven-footer. He had more ability on defense than he had on offense, but he could score points with the best of them. He was the national scoring leader in the 1945–46 season, and in the last home game he ever played, on February 22, 1946, against St. Louis University, he scored the highest single game total of his career, eclipsing a previous record. How many points? And whose previous record?

16. Kurland had a nickname that perfectly fit his height. What was it?

17. Kurland did not turn pro, but elected instead to play in the Olympics of 1948 and 1952, and with a leading amateur team of his day. Name this team. It was sponsored by an oil company for whom Kurland worked.

18. Grantland Rice bestowed the greatest of all amateur honors on Kurland. Name it.

19. Both Kurland and Mikan, because of their height and their remarkable ability to block shots on defense, were largely responsible for a new rule that is still in effect today. What rule?

20. Who were the "Cinderella Kids" of the 1943–44 season, and why that name?

21. Arizona won the Border Conference crown in 1946, but lost out in the quarterfinals of the NIT that year. Arizona's star player later became Secretary of the Interior in the cabinets of John F. Kennedy and Lyndon Johnson. Who was he?

22. One of basketball's all-time powerhouse college teams, Kentucky, had its own prominently promoted nickname in 1947–48. What was it?

23. That Kentucky team had a 6-foot-7-inch center whose older brother achieved fame as one of football's all-time great place kickers. Name these brothers. The younger brother played in the NBA for two years, scoring 2,925 points for Indianapolis.

ANSWERS

1. (a) Jim Thorpe; (b) Christy Mathewson; and (c) General Joseph "Vinegar Joe" Stilwell.

2. Byron "Whizzer" White, now a Justice of the United States Supreme Court.

3. In 1939 Hank Luisetti received $10,000 from Paramount Pictures to appear in a perfectly awful movie that is better left to oblivion. With the title of Campus Confessions, the movie featured Betty Grable as Luisetti's co-star. But she might just as well have been on another planet. "She didn't know I existed," Luisetti later admitted. "I never talked to her, and when I was supposed to kiss her, I couldn't bring myself to do it. It was horrible." Because he was presumably paid for playing basketball in the film, the Amateur Athletic Union placed Luisetti on suspension for one year.

4. After Pearl Harbor in December of 1941, Luisetti enlisted in the Navy. Not quite three years later, while still in the service, he developed spinal meningitis. Although he eventually recovered, he was told that he could never play basketball again. He was 28 years old at the time of his illness.

5. Nat Holman. Holman said of Luisetti's one-handed shooting technique: "I'll quit coaching if I have to teach one-handed shots to win . . . (It's) a shot predicated on a prayer. . . . There's only one way to shoot, the way we do it in the East—with two hands."

6. Elimination of the center jump after each score, and the 10-second rule, which requires that the offensive team bring the ball from the backcourt past the midcourt within 10 seconds or lose the ball to the other team.

7. "The Tall Firs."

8. Lou Boudreau.

9. *Chip Hilton is a fictional character created by Clair Bee, the great basketball coach and writer of sports fiction for young adults. Chip Hilton starred in every college sport in twenty-three books written by Clair Bee. Chip's basketball exploits were chronicled by Clair Bee in such books as "Hardcourt Upset," "Hoop Crazy," "Backboard Fever," "Backcourt Ace," and "Comeback Cager." Chip's coach was named Henry Rockwell, a thinly disguised version of Clair Bee himself.*

10. *DePaul University.*

11. *Mikan studied for the priesthood, but gave it up for basketball.*

12. *Ray Meyer, still going strong today, some thirty-five years later.*

13. *Oklahoma A. & M., now known as Oklahoma State University.*

14. *Henry "Hank" Iba.*

15. *Kurland scored 58 points, wiping out the previous record of 53 points held by George Mikan.*

16. *Kurland's nickname was "Foothills."*

17. *The Phillips 66ers, sponsored by the Phillips Oil Company.*

18. *Grantland Rice named Bob Kurland to his All-Time All-American team.*

19. *Goal-tending.*

20. *The Utah team of 1943–44 was known as the "Cinderella Kids" because they averaged only 18½ years in age. They lost in the first round of that season's NIT but received a special invitation to participate in the NCAA. They won the NCAA championship by defeating Dartmouth 42–40. Their freshman guard, Arnie Ferrin, was named the tournament's Most Valuable Player.*

21. *Stewart Udall.*

22. *"The Fabulous Five."*

23. *Kentucky's star center was Alex Groza, younger brother of football's great place kicker Lou Groza. That same team had another player with a famous athlete for a brother—Ralph Beard, brother of pro golfer Frank Beard.*

HALFTIME

The College Scandal of 1951

The sports world was shaken in 1919 by the "Black Sox" baseball scandal. In that notorious episode eight players of the American League's Chicago White Sox conspired to lose the World Series of 1919 to Cincinnati. The eight, including one of the most popular baseball players of that time, "Shoeless" Joe Jackson, were paid varying sums by gamblers to throw the Series. It was a scandal that no sports fan has ever forgotten.

Thirty-two years later another scandal involving bribery of athletes once again shook the sports world, but this time it was collegiate basketball that bore the shame. This was not the first instance of corruption in collegiate basketball ranks. In January of 1945 five players from Brooklyn College admitted they had accepted bribes to lose a game to Akron College. Four of the five players were immediately expelled from college. Nothing happened to the fifth because it was learned that he had never been registered as a student.

While this incident in 1945 was disturbing enough, it created no more than a ripple, for it appeared to be an isolated occurrence, a temporary aberration. Six years later, however, corruption of far more ominous proportions came to light, bringing with it shock and stunned disbelief. For this time it was not just a handful of players, but dozens; not just one game, but at least 86, in 23 cities and 17 states; not just one team, but seven. Even worse was the caliber of the teams. Included among the seven were the nation's top-ranked teams—schools that had already won both NCAA and NIT titles, or schools that had reached the tournament finals.

Evidence of the college basketball corruption of 1951 began to surface when a 6-foot 8-inch sophomore center from Manhattan College, Junius Kellogg, revealed to his coach in January that he had been offered $1,000 to control the point spread of a game between Manhattan and De-Paul. DePaul was favored to defeat Manhattan by 10 points. Kellogg's job would be to have a bad night so that Manhattan would lose by *more* than 10 points. Kellogg did not accept the bribe. As it happened, he *did* have a bad night against DePaul, but his replacement had a *hot* night, and Manhattan not only beat the 10-point spread, it beat DePaul as well, 62–59.

The point spread was invented by bookmakers to equalize the odds for bettors on basketball games. Prior to the point spread, the only way to bet on a basketball game was to play the odds—in other words, a superior team might be quoted at 8–5 over a weaker team. A bettor who wanted the superior team had to put up $8 to win $5, and vice versa for the weaker team. But weaker teams rarely won; bettors were reluctant to lay down a bet they would probably lose, even at good odds, and they were just as reluctant to put up more money to win less. Sometimes, in the case of an obvious mismatch, they might have to lay $5 just to win $1. This was not a satisfactory arrangement for bookmakers or for the bettors, both of whom wanted and needed action. It was then that the bookies came up with the point spread, or the "price," or the "line," as it was also called.

The point spread was simplicity itself. Instead of odds, a stronger team was now quoted as being so many points better than its weaker opponent. And just so there would be no confusion, a half point was added to the spread. On a ten-point spread (which actually would be 10½), if the weaker team lost by *less* than 10 points, anyone betting on that team would win. Example: in the Manhattan-DePaul game, if Manhattan had lost by a score of 62–53, all bets on Manhattan would have to be paid. Conversely, if DePaul had won by *more* than 10 points—62–51—all bets on Manhattan would be lost, and all bets on DePaul would be won.

It was this point spread arrangement that made it comparatively simple for gamblers to bribe collegiate players to fix, or "dump" certain games by shaving points. For the players, they had what they considered a reasonable rationale—they would not actually *lose* the game (especially if their team were the favorite, and that was generally the case with these fixes); all the players had to do was to *shave points*—win by *less* than the quoted spread so that the gamblers, who would be betting on the losing team, would actually wind up winning, since they would beat the spread.

For the many star players involved in these far-flung betting schemes, it wasn't too difficult to shave points, or even to lose outright if they had to. And almost no one could detect what they were doing. A half-second slower in going down the court, a misdirected pass to a teammate, a deliberate bad shot at the basket, failure to jump as high as an opponent for a rebound—a few of these during the course of a 40-minute college game could add up to enough to shave the proper number of points. And, more important for the players, no one would be the wiser. Coaches later admitted they had absolutely no idea that *their* players were shaving points, or even losing deliberately.

It all began to come apart when Junius Kellogg refused the gamblers' bait and reported the attempted bribe. His coach took Kellogg's information to the New York City district attorney. Soon after, five men were arrested—two former Manhattan College players and three gamblers. But the real stunner came a month later, when five players from another New York City team were arrested. These were local heroes—presumably untarnished and pure. They began talking, and the investigation spread. It was soon discovered that not only were games in the current season being fixed, but there had been fixes on games going back to 1947. Before the investigation was over that fall, dozens of careers were in ruins, some of the players went to prison, basketball schedules were cancelled or curtailed, and a few schools instituted athletics de-emphasis.

It was a shocker. One New York school official refused to believe that "our boys could do such a thing." A reporter answered that colleges were paying basketball players for campus jobs they didn't do and were giving passing grades for classes the players did not attend. In essence, the colleges were bribing the players to *play* basketball; gamblers were bribing these same players *not to play* up to their potential.

"What's the difference?" asked the reporter.

As for Junius Kellogg, he emerged from the scandals of 1951 a national hero. Sadly, his fame did him no good. After graduation from Manhattan College he joined a Harlem Globetrotter troupe in the fall of 1954 to barnstorm through the South and Southwest. As they were driving through Arkansas, right outside of Pine Bluff, their car had a blowout. The driver lost control, and the car turned over eight or ten times.

Kellogg was the only one injured. He was paralyzed from the waist down, and has been confined to a wheelchair ever since. But he has not forgotten basketball. He has coached wheelchair basketball, working with paraplegic veterans at the Bronx, New York, VA Hospital. Over the years, his wheelchair teams have so far won five world championships.

The sports world had thought it had seen the last of basketball fixing with the scandal of 1951. But another dumping scheme was uncovered in 1961, this time involving a former star player at Columbia who had become a successful lawyer, a prime wheeler-dealer, and a big-time fixer. This second major scandal implicated at least forty-seven players in forty-three known games. Most of the players escaped with their reputations intact. It was the former Columbia star, the most notorious of all, who proved to be the principal culprit. He received a stiff sentence for his part in the nationwide scheme to fix college games—four years in a federal prison.

That should have been the end of college basketball fixing, but another shocker came to light in January 1981, when it was announced that federal law enforcement officials had been investigating a possible point-shaving scheme at Boston College. Three Boston players were suspected of accepting bribes of $1,000 and $2,000 to shave points during the 1978–79 season. Although this new scandal appears to be limited to this one school, it nevertheless adds to the taint left over from the earlier schemes.

When the Fix Was In: The Players, the Games, the Coaches

1. On the night of February 17, 1951, New York's district attorney, Frank Hogan, announced that five members of a New York college basketball team were being questioned in connection with a point-rigging scheme. It was this announcement that stunned the basketball world. Name the school.

2. The year before, these same five players had been the darlings of New York City—unqualified heroes. Whenever they had trotted out onto the court of Madison Square Garden, their fans literally tore the house down with a battle cry that became famous across the entire country. What was that war cry?

3. This war cry was a corruption of a well-known French phrase. What phrase?

4. This enthusiastic shout turned to cries of dismay and shock when the full story of the 1951 corruption was made public. A second New York City area school was implicated in point shaving. What school?

5. When the coach of this second school heard that three of his players had been taken in for questioning, he placed a lamp in the window of his office so that the players could see it as they came back. "But at 6:00 A.M.," he said, "I went to the window and put out the light. They weren't coming back." Who was he?

6. In all, four New York area schools were implicated in the scandal. Aside from the two in the previous questions, which were the other two?

7. Meanwhile, other sections of the country were congratulating themselves on escaping the same corruption. One of the best-known coaches of all time piously proclaimed: "Out here in the Midwest this condition, of course, doesn't prevail." What coach?

8. Another renowned coach said about the gamblers who had managed, with comparative ease, to bribe New York area players: "They couldn't touch my boys with a ten-foot pole." What coach?

9. As it developed, both coaches were unhappily wrong. On July 24, 1951, it was disclosed that virtually the entire squad of a powerful Midwestern team, an active participant in the "grand-slam" season, had fixed at least three games of that season. And there had been rigging during the two preceding seasons. In all, seven players at this school were implicated. What school?

10. As for the coach with his ten-foot pole, he soon learned that even a *ten-inch* pole wouldn't have helped; his boys had been dumping games for years, including one in the NIT of 1949. That year he had hoped to be the first coach to win the "grand-slam;" his team did win the NCAA, but his boys betrayed him by losing in the quarter-finals of the NIT. Name his school.

11. Prior to the NIT, this team was considered to be the best in all of collegiate basketball. It had won 93 percent of its games over a four year period. In the 1948–49 season it won 29 of 30 games, and its last 21 in a row. It had gone into the quarter-finals of the NIT a solid ten-point favorite over its opponent. Yet it lost this game—as a result of rigging by three of its stars. They were supposed only to *shave points*, but they lost control of the game, and eventually lost the game itself Who beat them? By what score?

12. Two of these three star players, plus three other team-mates, were signed as a unit, upon graduation, to form a newly organized team in the NBA. They signed for a $50,000 bonus and a share of the profits, for they would be partial owners as well as players. What franchise?

13. Although many careers were ruined by the scandals of 1951, these two players probably lost more than anyone else. Their new franchise had been an immediate success, both on the court and at the box office. Each of the two was on his way to eminence in professional basketball, and at least one of them could well have been a genuine superstar. When they were arrested in October of 1951 and confessed to collegiate game fixing, they were immediately barred from the NBA for life, so they lost their ownership of a successful franchise and a bright future as players. Who were they? You've already encountered them in a previous question.

14. It was not only players who suffered. Two years after the 1951 revelations, a coach of one of the New York teams was suspended by his school for "conduct unbecoming a teacher," and "for neglect of duty." After much fighting on his part, he was eventually cleared of all charges and reinstated. Who was he? During his long tenure in New York sports he was affectionately known as "Mr. Basketball."

15. After the first arrests in February of 1951, the New York district attorney revealed that the seven players taken into custody at that point had received a total of $30,250 in bribes. Of that amount, $26,430 was recovered—all of it had been hidden away by the bribed players. Take a guess as to some of the not-so-ingenious hiding places these players used.

16. One fallout of the 1951 scandals had a peripheral effect upon Madison Square Garden. What was it?

17. Who was the star performer in the basketball scandal of 1961? After his release from prison, he continued to promote and live in a high fashion, using pornographic films as one base of his huge income. In 1975 his wheeling and dealing, his high living, and his life all came to a violent end when he was executed gangland style with a bullet through his head.

ANSWERS

1. *City College of New York.*

2. *"Allagaroo!" The complete cheer was "Allagaroo, garoo, garah; Allagaroo, garoo, garah; Ee-yah, Ee-yah, Sis, Boom, Bah!"*

3. *"À la guerre," which means "on to the war."*

4. *Long Island University.*

5. *Clair Bee.*

6. *Manhattan College and New York University.*

7. *Forrest C. "Phog" Allen.*

8. *Adolph Rupp.*

9. *Bradley.*

10. *Kentucky.*

11. *Loyola, 61–56.*

12. *Indianapolis.*

13. *Alex Groza and Frank Beard.*

14. *Nat Holman.*

15. *Some of the hiding places included safe deposit boxes taken out in the name of a player's mother or brother, envelopes sewn into the lining of a sports coat, an envelope taped to the back of a dresser drawer, and the toe of a shoe.*

16. *Because of the 1951 scandal, the NCAA recommended that Madison Square Garden never again be used for NCAA tournament games. Although it was a recommendation only, and not binding, no NCAA game since that time has ever been played in the Garden.*

17. *Jack Molinas*

THE THIRD PERIOD

The Modern Era—Colleges

1. Since CCNY's "grand-slam" of 1950 there have been five repeaters in the NIT—Bradley, Brigham Young, Dayton, Providence, and St. John's. One of these five won the NIT championship three times in that period. Which one?

2. From 1964 through 1975 UCLA (University of California at Los Angeles) seemed to own the NCAA tournament. How many NCAA championships did UCLA win all told in that period?

3. How many in a row?

4. What team stopped that win streak? When?

5. In its first NCAA win, UCLA defeated Duke University in a record-breaking performance. What record?

6. Between 1971 and 1974 UCLA established a modern record for consecutive wins without a loss. How many?

7. On January 19, 1974, that streak finally came to an end. Who finally snapped that streak? By what score?

8. In addition to UCLA, there have been four other repeaters in NCAA tournaments since the "grand-slam"—Cincinnati, Indiana, Kentucky, and San Francisco. Which of these four won three NCAA championships since 1950?

9. Who was their coach when they won all of their NCAA titles?

10. When he retired in 1972, in his forty-second year of

coaching, he had compiled the greatest number of wins by any college coach. How many?

11. UCLA has not been the only West Coast power. From 1954 through 1956 San Francisco set an earlier record for straight wins without a loss. How many did San Francisco win over those two seasons?

12. A Big Ten university, more noted for its perennially outstanding football teams, never won the NIT championship, but did win the NCAA once, in 1960. Name this Big Ten university.

13. Over the next two years, this same school was involved in two record-setting NCAA finals. What was so unusual about the finals of these two tournaments?

14. DePaul University has been consistently rated one of the top teams in the nation. How many NCAA or NIT titles has DePaul taken?

15. A five-time winner of the NCAA won the NIT only once since 1950. Name this 1976 NIT champion.

16. On March 4, 1970, Jacksonville University set a most unusual record. What was it?

17. Over the years, the following schools have been listed among the Top 20 in the country: Arkansas, Georgetown, Iowa, Louisiana State, Notre Dame, Oregon State, Syracuse, Texas A. & M., and Toledo. Which school in this group has never won either an NCAA or NIT championship?

18. What do these 10 schools have in common? Dayton, Duke, Florida State, Jacksonville, Kentucky, Memphis State, Michigan, North Carolina, Purdue, and Villanova.

19. One famous pre-season poll failed to include the eventual winners of both the 1980 NCAA and NIT titles among its Top 20. Who won the 1980 NCAA championship?

20. Who won the 1980 NIT title?

ANSWERS

1. *Bradley.*

2. *Ten.*

3. *Seven. From 1967 through 1973.*

4. *North Carolina State. In 1974.*

5. *On March 21, 1964, UCLA defeated Duke University to win its first NCAA title. The final score, 98–83, was the highest total ever recorded in an NCAA championship. The win gave UCLA an undefeated season of thirty victories.*

6. *UCLA won 88 games in a row, setting a record that may prove very hard to beat.*

7. *Notre Dame finally stopped that win streak on January 19, 1974, defeating UCLA by a heart-stopping score of 71–70. Oddly, Notre Dame was the last team to beat UCLA, in 1970, by a score of 89–82. After that, for four years, no one else was able to stop the UCLA machine until Notre Dame did it again in a nationally televised game in 1974. With 21 seconds left to play, UCLA had a lead of 70–69, but Notre Dame's Dwight Clay put his team ahead to stay with a shot from the corner, and UCLA's remarkable streak came to an end.*

8. *Kentucky.*

9. *Adolph Rupp.*

10. *His teams won 874 games out of 1,064, for a winning percentage of .821. As Rupp himself saw it, no other college coach will ever come close to matching that total. He once said this about young coaches he called "whippersnappers": "I see these young coaches come along with theories opposite to mine. So I go to the farm and think things over. Then I figure out that if these* *coaches begin at the age of 25 and win at least 20 games a year—then it's still going to be 45 years before they'll be able to match me in wins."*

11. *Fifty-five.*

12. *Ohio State.*

13. *In 1961 and 1962 Ohio State met Cincinnati in the finals of the NCAA tournaments for both years. It was the first and only time that two teams from the same state played each other in the finals of two consecutive NCAA tournaments. Cincinnati won both times—70–65 in 1961, and 71–59 in 1962.*

14. *DePaul University has never won an NCAA tournament. It did win the NIT once, in 1945. George Mikan, its great star, scored 34 of DePaul's 71 points in that tournament. He was named the tournament's Most Valuable Player.*

15. *Kentucky.*

16. *On March 4, 1970, Jacksonville defeated Miami University by a score of 101–97. Jacksonville thus became the first college team to average more than 100 points a game for an entire season.*

17. *None of these teams has ever won either an NCAA or NIT title, although many of them have made it to the tournaments.*

18. *They all lost to UCLA in the NCAA finals.*

19. *The 1980 NCAA champion was Louisville.*

20. *Virginia won the 1980 NIT title.*

Time out: Collegiate Odds and Ends

1. In the 1953–54 season, scoring by major college basketball teams reached a new peak. One player from a major college scored 50 or more points eight separate times, and 100 points in a single game. Who was he? And name his school.

2. This same player holds two other collegiate records, both set in that same season. What records?

3. The name Bevo Francis may mean nothing to you, but *he* holds what may well be an unbeatable collegiate record for scoring the most points in a single game. How many points?

4. When San Francisco had its record-setting seasons in 1954–55 and 1955–56, it was led by 6-foot 10-inch Bill Russell. His style of play brought a totally new dimension to basketball. How?

5. Wilt Chamberlain holds many professional records, more than any other pro player. How many college records does he have?

6. Pete Maravich holds more individual NCAA records than any other collegiate player, among them the most career points scored. Name two other all-time NCAA career records he holds.

7. During the 1968–69 season Maravich averaged a record 43.8 points per game, and thus became the second sophomore to lead the nation in scoring. Who was the first?

8. Another sophomore, 6-foot 3-inch Ronnie Carr of Western Carolina University, scored another first when he was honored in 1980 by the Basketball Hall of Fame. What did he do to be so recognized?

9. One of the most controversial games ever played took place during the summer Olympics of 1972. The United States lost that game 51–50, but refused the silver medals that were awarded to them as runners–up. Who beat them, and why did the United States refuse its second-place medals?

10. A few years later, in the late summer of 1979, a United States team did much better at the World University Games in Mexico City when it rolled up scores of 145–21 and 173–14. Who were the unfortunate victims in these two games?

11. In a recent survey it was determined that the state of Kentucky, with a ratio of one college basketball game attended per 3.31 Kentuckians, and the state of Indiana, with one game attended per 4.66 Indianans, had the best per capita attendance records in the nation. But a senator from a western state insisted that *his* state had the best per capita attendance record. What state? And what was his estimate?

12. Who made the longest shot ever recorded? And how long was it?

13. UCLA holds the record for the most consecutive victories. What school holds the record for the most wins in a perfect season?

14. What two teams hold the NCAA record for the most points scored in a single game?

15. What do Lew Alcindor, Spencer Haywood, Pete Maravich, Rick Mount, and Calvin Murphy have in common?

ANSWERS

1. *Frank Selvy. He played for Furman University of Green-ville, South Carolina.*

2. *Selvy holds the NCAA records for the most free throws attempted in a single season, 444, and the most free throws made in one season, 355; both records were set in 1954 and have yet to be equalled or broken.*

3. *Bevo Francis scored 113 points on February 3, 1954, in a game between his school, Rio Grande of Jackson, Ohio, and Hillsdale, Michigan. Rio Grande won that game 134–91, which meant that all of his teammates combined scored only 21 points to his 113.*

4. *Bill Russell was a superb blocker and defensive player. When San Francisco won its two consecutive NCAA titles, it led the nation in defense by allowing only 52.1 points per game in 1954–55, and 52.2 points a game the following season. Since then, Russell's style of defense has become an integral part of the game. Some years later, when Dave DeBusschere was a Knick, he said this about Russell's influence on basketball: "In the fifties, basketball was a power game with big muscle men around the basket. . . . There wasn't much finesse. . . . Then along came . . . Russell who controlled the inside. . . . The concept of team defense resulted from big men cutting off the traditional way of scoring. You had to learn how to defense guys [like] Russell."*

5. *Wilt Chamberlain holds no NCAA college records. He himself blamed his collegiate opponents for "freezing the ball," and thus denying him the chance to do more scoring. He said this about his college career: "I averaged 30 points a game and hit almost 50 percent of my shots, but with the other teams freezing the ball, I couldn't get enough shots to score more. I averaged* *about 16 rebounds a game, too, but how do you get rebounds when the other team won't shoot? We had one game against Oklahoma State where they passed the ball 160 times before taking a shot!"*

6. *Highest scoring average, 44.2; and most field goals, 1,387.*

7. *Oscar Robertson, during the 1957–58 season, when he averaged 35.1 points per game.*

8. *The Basketball Hall of Fame honored Ronnie Carr for being the first college basketball player to make a three-point field goal. The Southern Conference, of which Carr's school, Western Carolina University, is a member, agreed to experiment with the three point field goal for 101 games of the 1980–81 season, including nonleague games and a postseason tournament. Three points are awarded for a shot made from outside a half circle with a radius of 22 feet from the basket.*

9. *In the 1972 summer Olympics the United States team, which had won 62 consecutive games in Olympic competition, was matched in the finals against the USSR. With only seconds left to play, the United States was leading 50–49. Because of various misunderstandings among the referees, coaches, timers, and other officials, the Russian team was given three chances to play the final seconds. On the third chance, the USSR scored what was eventually recorded as the winning basket, giving the game and the gold medal to Russia by a score of 51–50. The United States claimed that time had already expired when that last basket was made. When their claim was rejected the United States players refused the silver medals   .*

10. *The United States defeated Saudı Arabia, 145–21, and Sudan, 173–14.*

11. *Republican Senator Orrin G. Hatch of Utah claimed that his state had a ratio of one game attended per 1.74 citizens. Out of a population of 1,268,000, Utah had a total collegiate basketball attendance of 728,805.*

12. *The longest shot was made by Les Henson of Virginia Tech on January 21, 1980, when he fired a buzzer shot practically the entire length of the floor. The shot was officially recorded at 89 feet, 3 inches. The previous record was 88 feet, set by Rudy Williams of Providence, on February 17, 1979.*

13. The record for the most wins in a perfect season is 32, held jointly by North Carolina, 1957, and Indiana, 1976.

14. Nevada-Las Vegas and Hawaii-Hilo. On February 19, 1976, they scored a total of 275 points—Nevada-Las Vegas, 164, and Hawaii-Hilo, 111.

15. All five of them were consensus All-American in 1968–69.

Play Resumes: College All-Stars

1. Match the following NBA stars with their colleges:

(A) Rick Barry		(a)	Cincinnati
(B) Elgin Baylor		(b)	Florida State
(C) Bill Bradley		(c)	Grambling
(D) Wilt Chamberlain		(d)	Holy Cross
(E) Bob Cousy		(e)	Kansas
(F) Dave Cowens		(f)	Louisville
(G) Julius Erving		(g)	Massachusetts
(H) Earl Monroe		(h)	Miami of Florida
(I) Willis Reed		(i)	Princeton
(J) Oscar Robertson		(j)	Seattle
(K) Wes Unseld		(k)	West Virginia
(L) Jerry West		(l)	Winston-Salem

2. This collegiate basketball player from Duke University was a rarity—he made All-American in *two* sports, baseball *and* basketball. As a 6-foot, 180-pound guard, he won the NCAA scoring title in 1950–51 with 831 points in 31 games, a single-season scoring record. But he went on to greater fame as a shortstop with the Pittsburgh Pirates. He won both the batting championship and the National League's MVP award in 1960. Name him.

3. Louisiana State University has had two superstars in the NBA. The more recent is Pete Maravich. Who was the other?

4. Ohio State had two future greats of the NBA on one team at the same time, 1959–1962. One of them was John Havlicek. Name the other.

5. Two of the outstanding centers of all time played for UCLA during the years of its NCAA mastery. Who were they?

6. For three years the UCLA team was nicknamed for the second of these two star centers. What nickname?

7. Which of these two giants is the taller?

8. UCLA had one-half of another distinctive pair, a star father-and-son combination. The son played for UCLA from 1977 to 1980, and the father played for Cornell, 1945–49. Name this star father-son combination.

9. In one of the most famous college games ever played, 52,693 fans jammed into Houston's Astrodome on January 20, 1968 to watch the "Big A" and the "Big E" battle one another. Who were these two college superstars, and what schools did they represent?

10. Who won that titanic contest? By what score?

11. When this eventual NBA superstar first enrolled at the University of Kansas in 1956, Coach Phog Allen said this about his team's prospects: "With him, we'll never lose a game; we could win the national championship with [him], two sorority girls, and two Phi Beta Kappas." Who was he talking about? And was he right?

12. Which of the following won the NCAA Outstanding Player Award for two consecutive years? Lew Alcindor, Elgin Baylor, Wilt Chamberlain, Jerry Lucas, Pete Maravich, Oscar Robertson, Bill Russell, Bill Walton, Jerry West.

13. Who was the first college player to score more than 2,000 points in two seasons?

14. Who holds the record for the highest field goal percentage in a single season?

15. Who held the previous record, and when w⸱⸱s ⸱t set?

16. In March of 1979 two of the most publicized college players of the past decade faced each other in the finals of the NCAA tournament in Salt Lake City. Name these two players.

17. What schools did they play for?

18. Which school took the 1979 NCAA title? By what score?

19. These two players are now in the NBA. Who do they play for?

20. One of them was signed for the largest rookie salary ever paid. Which one, and how much was he paid?

ANSWERS

1. *(A-h)   Rick Barry, Miami of Florida*
   (B-j)   Elgin Baylor, Seattle
   (C-i)   Bill Bradley, Princeton
   (D-e)   Wilt Chamberlain, Kansas
   (E-d)   Bob Cousy, Holy Cross
   (F-b)   Dave Cowens, Florida State
   (G-g)   Julius Erving, Massachusetts
   (H-l)   Earl Monroe, Winston-Salem
   (I-c)   Willis Reed, Grambling
   (J-a)   Oscar Robertson, Cincinnati
   (K-f)   Wes Unseld, Louisville
   (L-k)   Jerry West, West Virginia

2. *Dick Groat.*

3. *Bob Pettit.*

4. *Jerry Lucas.*

5. *Lew Alcindor and Bill Walton.*

6. *"The Walton Gang."*

7. *Lew Alcindor (now known as Kareem Abdul-Jabbar) is the taller at 7 feet 2 inches. Bill Walton is 6 feet 11 inches.*

8. *Father, Ernest Vandeweghe II; son, Ernest "Kiki" Vandeweghe III. The father is a doctor practicing in California, and Kiki is now playing forward for the NBA's Dallas Mavericks. He was a first-round draft pick for this expansion team.*

9. *The "Big A" was Lew Alcindor, UCLA; the "Big E" was Elvin Hayes, Houston.*

10. *Houston defeated UCLA, 71–69. At the time, UCLA had another win streak going. Houston stopped it at 47 wins.*

11. *Wilt Chamberlain. No, Coach Allen was not right. In Chamberlain's sophomore year Kansas lost in the NCAA finals to North Carolina. In Chamberlain's junior year, when he was a unanimous All-American, Kansas failed to reach either the NCAA or the NIT finals. Chamberlain did not return to school for his senior year, but turned pro by joining the Harlem Globetrotters in 1958.*

12. *Jerry Lucas, in 1960 and 1961.*

13. *Pete Maravich, from 1967–68 through 1969, his sophomore and junior years. He scored a total of 2,286 points.*

14. *Steve Johnson of Oregon State had a field goal percentage of .746 in 1981.*

15. *Steve Johnson. He had a percentage of .710 in 1980.*

16. *Earvin "Magic" Johnson and Larry Bird.*

17. *Earvin Johnson, Michigan State; Larry Bird, Indiana State.*

18. *Michigan State won the 1979 NCAA title, 75–64.*

19. *Magic Johnson plays for the Los Angeles Lakers, and Larry Bird plays for the Boston Celtics.*

20. *Larry Bird became the highest-paid rookie so far when he signed with the Celtics in 1979 for a reported $650,000 per year.*

THE FOURTH PERIOD

The NBA

Big-league basketball as we now know it began in the fall of 1946. With the end of World War II, many outstanding collegiate players who had been in the armed forces became available for professional play. And the lifting of wartime restrictions left Americans with money to spend on entertainment. But professional basketball was limited to a midwestern group, the National Basketball League, and to a weekend eastern circuit that was originally called the American Basketball League (it later changed its name to the Eastern League). Most fan interest was still centered on college basketball, which continued to draw enthusiastic crowds, primarily in college gymnasiums.

A number of large arenas in major eastern cities were devoted during the winter months to hockey, which was even then a major sport. But these arenas were frequently dark when the home hockey team was on the road. (The exception was Madison Square Garden, with its college basketball games to take up the slack time.) Ice shows, such as those made popular by Sonja Henie, stayed in each city only for a couple of weeks and then moved on. The arena operators and owners of the hockey clubs wanted another attraction to fill their houses on vacant nights. What better attraction than big-league pro basketball?

Such an idea was first suggested by Max Kase, a sportswriter for the *New York Journal American*. A half-dozen men, representing varied ice-hockey and arena interests, ·agreed with Kase, and met in New York City on June 6, 1946, to organize the forerunner of the present NBA. With an eleven-city lineup, they called their new league the

Basketball Association of America (the BAA). Among those at that historic meeting were Ned Irish of Madison Square Garden and Walter Brown, president of the Boston Garden.

Ned Irish was less enthusiastic about pro basketball than the others, for the Garden continued to have a spectacular success with its college programs. Including its regular season double-headers, the NIT, the NCAA Tournament (which was then being played in New York), and the East-West All-Star game, Garden collegiate basketball drew 528,000 spectators in 1946. Ned Irish did not need anything else, but he was shrewd enough to realize that pro basketball had a future, and he was not about to let it pass him by. And he knew that without New York City no professional major sport could hope to succeed.

For their first commissioner, the six arena representatives selected Maurice Podoloff, a lawyer and banker who was president of the American Hockey League. Five feet two inches tall and almost as round, Podoloff knew exactly nothing about basketball. But that didn't matter. The new owners didn't know much about it either, with the exception of Ned Irish, whose basketball experience had been limited to college teams. Podoloff's principal task was to keep the new league alive and thriving.

He succeeded admirably, although not without a struggle. First of all, the BAA had formidable opposition from the NBL, the National Basketball League, with franchises in midwestern cities ranging from Chicago to Detroit to Fort Wayne to Sheboygan to Anderson, Indiana. The NBL had a major star in George Mikan, while the BAA had no established stars of Mikan's stature. And the BAA had additional competition from the weekend Eastern League, which included Edward Gottlieb's Sphas and other teams in large eastern cities.

Podoloff and the new BAA persisted, despite its stiff competition from college basketball and from the existing pro leagues. During its early years the BAA lost one franchise after another, for lack of fan support, lack of money, and lack of suitable talent. But as the BAA lost teams, Podoloff lured replacements away from the two rival leagues, especially from the NBL. In 1949–50, the BAA merged with the remnants of the NBL to become the NBA, the National Basketball Association, with seventeen teams. It now had George Mikan, playing for the NBA's Minneapolis Lakers. And other defections from the Eastern League weakened that group considerably. The NBA at last had full-time pro basketball all to itself. Although collegiate basketball continued to remain a major draw, the NBA prospered, for fan interest in pro basketball was beginning to grow, despite constant loss of franchises and shifts of other franchises from one city to another.

In 1961 Abe Saperstein decided the time was right to organize a new pro rival, the American Basketball League, a name he appropriated from the defunct circuit of twenty or thirty years before. His ABL, however, did no better than its predecessors, and folded after less than two seasons.

It was not until 1967, with the formation of the American Basketball Association (the ABA), that the NBA had any serious competition.

What happened between the NBA and the ABA is a story in itself. In the meantime, let's concentrate on the early days of the NBA.

The Early Years

1. Of the BAA's eleven charter members, only two are still in existence—the New York Knicks and the Boston Celtics. Match the team names of the other nine original BAA members to the city that each represented.

(A) Chicago		(a) Bombers
(B) Cleveland		(b) Capitols
(C) Detroit		(c) Falcons
(D) Philadelphia		(d) Huskies
(E) Pittsburgh		(e) Ironmen
(F) Providence		(f) Rebels
(G) St. Louis		(g) Stags
(H) Toronto		(h) Steamrollers
(I) Washington		(i) Warriors

2. The first game in the new BAA was played on November 1, 1946, in Toronto. Who was Toronto's opponent? And who won, by what score?

3. With a schedule of 60 regular season games and a play-off format similar to hockey's, the BAA ended its first season, 1946–47, with Washington on top of the six-team Eastern Division, and Chicago as champions of the five-team Western Division. But neither team won the eventual playoff title. Who were the first BAA champs?

4. Who won the *second* BAA title? (This was for the season of 1947–48.)

5. What team won the first *NBA* championship? (For the 1949–50 season, when the BAA officially became the NBA.)

6. Who was the first team to win two consecutive NBA titles? Watch this one.

7. In the 1947–48 season, George Mikan and the Minneapolis Lakers were in the NBL. Mikan won the NBL scoring title for 1947–48 with 1,195 points in 56 games, and a 21.3 average per game. Who won the BAA scoring title for that same season? The BAA, in its second season of play, reduced the number of games for each team to 48, but returned to a 60-game format the following season.

8. The BAA's first superstar was a 6-foot 6-inch ex-Marine who had seen action on Iwo Jima and Guam during World War II. He had played college ball for a small school in Kentucky, Murray State. He became a BAA rookie at the age of 26 and zoomed to instant stardom with the help of adroit publicity boosted by his own superlative playmaking. Name him. It may help you to know that he played for Edward Gottlieb, who had been lured away from the Sphas to coach in the BAA. Gottlieb's team, as it happened, won the first BAA title.

9. As the New York Yankees became a baseball dynasty, and UCLA emerged as a collegiate basketball dynasty, so too did the Boston Celtics dominate professional basketball for a number of years. But there was an earlier pro-basketball dynasty before the Celtics. What team?

10. There have been many close and exciting games that can qualify on anybody's list of the ten best. But one game that must rank with any of them took place on March 21, 1953, during the first round of the 1953 NBA playoffs. There were four overtimes, 106 personal fouls, players fighting players, and players fighting the police. Not only were the 106 personal fouls a playoff record, but so was the total of 12 players who fouled out. When the final buzzer mercifully ended this wild brawl, the winning team had won by six points. Who were the two teams involved, and what was the final score?

11. Another memorable game, this one distinguished in the opposite direction—for its dullness—ended with a score of 19–18, the lowest in NBA history. Who played that game, when, and who won?

12. These two games were partially responsible for two significant rule changes that helped to speed up the action, and reduce the personal fouls that threatened to take the fun out of basketball. What were these two rule changes, and when were they made?

13. With these new rules in effect, action was faster and scoring was higher. On February 27, 1959, a team scored 173 points for a new NBA record—the most points scored by one team in a single game. Name that team.

14. Three years later, on March 2, 1962, two other teams scored a total of 316 points for another record—the most points scored in a single game by two teams. Name those two teams.

15. This record was matched eight years later, on March 12, 1970, by two more teams. Name them.

ANSWERS

1. (A-g) Chicago Stags
   (B-f) Cleveland Rebels
   (C-c) Detroit Falcons
   (D-i) Philadelphia Warriors
   (E-e) Pittsburgh Ironmen
   (F-h) Providence Steamrollers
   (G-a) St. Louis Bombers
   (H-d) Toronto Huskies
   (I-b) Washington Capitols

2. The New York Knicks defeated the Toronto Huskies, 68–66. To hype the gate, Toronto gave free admission to any fan taller than its 6-foot 8-inch George Nostrand. All others had to pay from seventy-five cents to two-and-a-half dollars.

3. The Philadelphia Warriors.

4. The Baltimore Bullets.

5. The Minneapolis Lakers.

6. The Minneapolis Lakers. They won the BAA title in 1948–49, and the first NBA title in 1949–50.

7. The BAA scoring title for the 1947–48 season was divided—Max Zaslofsky of the Chicago Stags scored the most points, 1,009; the highest scoring average went to Joe Fulks of the Philadelphia Warriors—22.1 average per game.

8. Joe Fulks. In his first year in the BAA, 1946–47, he literally went wild. He shot more times, 1,557, and scored more baskets, 475, than anyone else. He finished the season with 1,389 points, 400 more than his nearest competitor, with an average per game of 23.2.

9. *The Minneapolis Lakers. In the first eight years of the BAA/NBA, the Lakers won five titles, three of them in succession, 1951–52 through 1953–54*

10. *The Boston Celtics and the Syracuse Nationals. Boston won that game in the fourth overtime, 111–105. That win sent Boston into the semifinals, where they lost to the New York Knicks, three games out of four.*

11. *On November 22, 1950, the Fort Wayne Pistons defeated the Minneapolis Lakers, 19–18, for the lowest combined score in NBA history. Ironically, both Fort Wayne and Minneapolis made it to the 1950–51 playoffs, but neither team reached the final round.*

12. *In 1954 the 24-second rule was adopted. This rule requires a team that gains possession of the ball to shoot within 24 seconds or turn the ball over to the other team. As the Fort Wayne-Minneapolis game proved, stalling was frequently the result when one team pulled ahead and deliberately froze the ball to keep the other team from shooting. But the 24-second rule eliminated such tactics. The other rule change awarded free bonus throws after four personal fouls per quarter per team. The Boston-Syracuse game of March 21, 1953, with its 106 personal fouls, showed what could happen when a team was willing to trade one point—all that was then allowed for any personal foul—for a chance to get the ball back after the free throw and perhaps make two points. The new foul rule eliminated that tactic. Under this change, a player who was fouled in an ordinary one-shot situation was given a bonus throw or a chance to make two points instead of one, and in a two-shot situation, being fouled in the act of shooting for example, the fouled player was given three chances to make two points. These new rules—the 24-second clock and the bonus shots after four team fouls per quarter—eliminated all chances of stalling, which had led only to boredom for the fans. Pro basketball became a truly professional major sport—fast and exciting.*

13. *On February 27, 1959, Boston scored 173 points against Minneapolis to set a new NBA record. Minneapolis itself scored 139 points, normally more than enough to win.*

14. *On March 2, 1962, 316 points were scored by Philadelphia and New York—Philadelphia 169, New York 147*

15. *This record total was matched on March 12, 1970, by Cincinnati and San Diego—Cincinnati 165, San Diego 151.*

Time Out: NBA Stats, Etc.

1. During the 1950–51 season George Mikan scored 1,932 points for a record single-season performance. But seven years later that mark was wiped out when a player from the Detroit Pistons scored 2,001 points to become the first man in NBA history to score more than 2,000 points in one season. Name him.

2. Who was the first player to score 10,000 career points?

3. Who was the first player to score 15,000 career points?

4. The NBA's Rookie of the Year was chosen for the first time in 1953. Who was the first Rookie of the Year?

5. Who was the first NBA rookie to make the All-NBA team in his rookie year?

6. The Maurice Podoloff Cup, named for the NBA's first commissioner, was established in 1955–56 as an award for the NBA's Most Valuable Player. Who was the first recipient of the Podoloff Cup?

7. In 1959–60 the award for Rookie of the Year and the Podoloff Cup for Most Valuable Player were both won by the same man for the first time. Name him.

8. Since then, that feat has been repeated only once. Name the second NBA player to win both awards in the same year.

9. Who was the first player to win the Podoloff Cup twice?

10. Who was the first player to win the Podoloff Cup in two consecutive seasons?

11. Who was the first player to win the Podoloff Cup in *three* successive seasons?

12. Only one other player has ever been named Most Valuable Player for three successive seasons. Name him.

13. Paul Arizin, an All-American from Villanova, starred in the NBA for 10 seasons, from 1950–51 through 1961–62, playing all that time for the same team. He had 16,266 career points, with an overall average of 22.8 points per game. He scored in four figures for each of his 10 seasons, and was named to the All-NBA team three times. What team did he play for?

14. Arizin won the NBA scoring title in 1951–52 with a total of 1,674 points and an average of 25.4 points per game. But the scoring title was won in the next three years by one of his teammates. Who was he?

15. Practically synonymous with pro basketball is the name Red Auerbach, a long-time coach and general manager of the Boston Celtics. But he did not begin his coaching career with the Celtics. What was his first pro coaching job?

16. The first coach of the Boston Celtics, one of two who preceded Auerbach, had a long career in pro basketball. He was one of the great pros during the 1920s and 1930s, appearing in over 3,200 games, many of them with the Cleveland Rosenblums. He coached Seton Hall University of South Orange, New Jersey, to 294 wins, including one stretch of 44 straight. In two seasons with the Celtics, he did not do quite as well, winning only 42 against 66 losses. Who was he? He was named to the Basketball Hall of Fame in 1964.

17. When the owners of the recent expansion team, the Dallas Mavericks, purchased their franchise, it was reported they paid the NBA $12,000,000 for the privilege. And a move to establish an NBA franchise in Vancouver, Canada, would have cost those owners $16,000,000. In the early years of the BAA, when teams were folding one after the other, franchises could have been purchased for comparative pennies. When the owners of the original Philadelphia Warriors, one of the eleven charter members of the BAA, decided they wanted out, they sold their franchise to their coach. Who was he, and how much did he pay for the Warriors?

18. Why was the number 24 selected for the 24-second clock? Why not 25 seconds, or 26, or 22?

19. The free-throw lane began as a keyhole, 6 feet wide, with a large circle at the top. The lane was later changed to 12 feet, and is now 16 feet wide. (It is still referred to as the key or keyhole although it may no longer look like one.) Why was it widened?

20. If you were asked to name one of the early greats in the NBA, you would probably answer Bob Cousy or George Mikan. But there were others who are considered among the all-time great pros—"Easy Ed" Macauley, Jim Pollard, Bill Sharman, and Jack Twyman, to mention four. Match these players with their teams and their positions.

ANSWERS

1. George Yardley of the Detroit Pistons was the first player to score 2,000 or more points in a single season. He set his mark in 1957–58. His average of 27.8 for that season was second only to Mikan's 28.4, established in 1950–51. Mikan's earlier records were made in 68 games, while Yardley appeared in 72 games for his record.

2. George Mikan. In his eighth season of play, 1953–54, he scored 1,306 points to bring his total to over 10,000. He retired at the end of that season, but tried a comeback two years later. He was out of condition and overweight, and no longer the greatest player of his time. He scored only 390 points in his final season, for a career total of 11,764.

3. Dolph Schayes of the Syracuse Nationals. The 6-foot 8-inch center finished the 1959–60 season with 15,798 career points. He played for four more years, ending with a career total of 19,247.

4. Don Meineke of the Fort Wayne Pistons.

5. Alex Groza of the Indianapolis Jets. He was named to the All-NBA team in 1949–50, his rookie season. He was again named to the All-NBA team for his second and last year in the NBA—1950–51. He was arrested in October of 1951 during the collegiate basketball scandal of that year. When he confessed that he had been involved in game-fixing, he was barred from professional basketball for life.

6. The first recipient of the Maurice Podoloff Cup was Bob Pettit of the St. Louis Hawks.

7. Wilt Chamberlain, Philadelphia Warriors.

8. Wes Unseld of the Baltimore Bullets, in 1968–69.

[128]

9. *Bob Pettit, 1955–56 and 1958–59.*

10. *Bill Russell, Boston Celtics. He was named Most Valuable Player in 1960–61 and 1961–62.*

11. *Bill Russell. He won the Podoloff Cup for the third straight time in 1962–63.*

12. *Wilt Chamberlain. He was named Most Valuable Player for three successive seasons, 1965–66 through 1967–68.*

13. *The Philadelphia Warriors.*

14. *Neil Johnston.*

15. *With the Washington Capitols. Red began his coaching career as a high-school coach in Washington, D.C., when he was only 23. After service in the Navy during World War II, he jumped directly to the pros in 1946 at the age of 29. Auerbach was elected to the Hall of Fame in 1968.*

16. *John "Honey" Russell.*

17. *Edward Gottlieb purchased the Philadelphia Warriors for a reported $25,000. He sold the team in 1962 for $850,000. The new owners moved the franchise to San Francisco, where the team became the San Francisco Warriors and eventually the Golden State Warriors.*

18. *Danny Biasone, owner of the Syracuse Nationals, was the man who proposed the 24-second clock. He arrived at 24 seconds by dividing the number of shots taken in typical games into the time played. At 48 minutes per game—or 2,880 seconds—24 seconds per shot meant 120 shots, 60 for each team. Dividing 2,880 by any other number—22 seconds, or 23, or 25, or 26—gave an unbalanced result: 115.2 shots per game at 25 seconds per shot, as one example. Two thousand, eight hundred and eighty can be evenly divided by 20, but 20 seconds seemed too restrictive, so the new 24-second clock was adopted by the NBA owners on April 22, 1954.*

19. *The free-throw lane was widened to neutralize the height advantage of superb tall players like Bill Russell and Wilt Chamberlain. Since no offensive player can stay in the free-throw lane longer than 3 seconds while his team has control of the ball, a shot has to be taken from the keyhole within that very short time span, or the offensive player must move out of the key. When the* free-throw lane was only 6 feet wide, as it was for many years, it was comparatively easy for a good tall man to shoot from that distance. Now that the lane is 16 feet wide, it's a lot tougher, and requires more accuracy. It should be noted that the NBA now has dozens of players as tall as or taller than Bill Russell, and some even taller than Wilt Chamberlain.

20. "Easy Ed" Macauley, 6-foot 8-inch center, played for St. Louis and Boston, 1949 through 1959; Jim Pollard, 6-foot 3-inch guard for the Minneapolis Lakers, 1947 through 1955; Bill Sharman, 6-foot 1-inch guard for Washington and Boston, from 1950 through 1961; and Jack Twyman, 6-foot 6-inch forward for Rochester and Cincinnati, 1955 through 1966.

Play Resumes: The ABA, the Merger and the NBA Today

In February 1967 the American Basketball Association was organized to compete with the NBA. Whether by design or accident, the new league began with the same number of charter members as had the BAA—11. The ABA began play in the fall of 1967, with two major innovations. First, it had the three-point field goal for shots made from 25 feet or more; and second, it used a red, white, and blue basketball, proposed by its new commissioner. (One critic unkindly suggested that the new ball would look good only on the nose of a seal.)

But the ABA needed superstars. All they had were NBA rejects, so they began an aggressive campaign to lure top players from the NBA. They had their first and most notable success with Rick Barry of the San Francisco Warriors.

In 1966–67, Barry's second year in the pros, he led NBA scoring with 2,775 points and a 35.6 average. He decided to jump to the ABA to play for Oakland, the Warriors' Bay Area rival. He may have been influenced by the fact that the Oakland coach was his father-in-law. Whatever the reason for his decision, it cost him a year of competition. The San Francisco Warriors sued to bring Rick Barry back. The courts ruled that Barry could stay with Oakland, but would have to sit out the 1967–68 season.

When Barry began playing again, in 1968–69, he showed that he had been worth waiting for. He averaged 34 points a game even though he appeared only in 35 games because of an injury.

The ABA persuaded other NBA stars to make the jump—Zelmo Beaty, the 6-foot 9-inch center of the St. Louis

Hawks, for one. And ABA teams went after promising collegians with a generous checkbook. They outbid the NBA for the services of Mel Daniels, All-American first-round draft choice from New Mexico, and signed sophomore Spencer Haywood from the University of Detroit.

For its part, the NBA countered by trying to lure ABA players to join the NBA, or by lavishing their own huge payments on college stars. They outbid the ABA for Lew Alcindor, Pete Maravich, and Bob Lanier.

The bidding battle became a bidding war; bonuses and contracts escalated, with collegiate superstars the lucky recipients. In their zeal to grab the finest available talent, both the ABA and the NBA threatened to bankrupt themselves, and they finally realized that the bidding war had gotten out of hand. They spoke of a merger, but nothing came of the merger talks.

The ABA continued signing young new stars—Artis Gilmore of Jacksonville University, Jim McDaniels from Western Kentucky University, Julius Erving from the University of Massachusetts, and George McGinnis from Indiana University, and in one unusual and controversial case, eighteen-year-old Moses Malone directly out of high school.

Despite lawsuits back and forth between the ABA and the NBA—each accusing the other of raiding—the ABA appeared to be on the road to respectability. In 1971–72 almost three million fans turned out for ABA games. But many ABA franchises were in trouble. And ABA superstars began returning or jumping to the NBA—Rick Barry went back to the Warriors, and Spencer Haywood signed with the NBA's Seattle SuperSonics. By 1975–76 the end was in sight for the ABA; too many top players had defected to the opposition, and too many clubs were folding—only seven teams were left, in one division.

At the end of the 1975–76 season, after nine years and millions of dollars, the ABA owners finally gave up. Three of the seven teams disbanded and the remaining four were absorbed into an expanded NBA, which had previously realigned itself into two conferences and four divisions.

Once again the NBA had outlived all serious competition.

Although there is no guarantee that the present NBA lineup of 23 teams will last forever—basketball franchises seem to come and go with depressing regularity—the NBA is nevertheless more solidly entrenched today than ever as the only major professional basketball league.

THE ABA

1. Of the 11 ABA charter members, only one, the Indiana Pacers, survives in its original franchise with its original name. Match the team names of the other ten charter clubs with the cities or areas they represented.

(A)	Anaheim	(a)	Americans
(B)	Dallas	(b)	Amigos
(C)	Denver	(c)	Buccaneers
(D)	Houston	(d)	Chaparrals
(E)	Kentucky	(e)	Colonels
(F)	Minnesota	(f)	Mavericks
(G)	New Jersey	(g)	Muskies
(H)	New Orleans	(h)	Oaks
(I)	Oakland	(i)	Pipers
(J)	Pittsburgh	(j)	Rockets

2. Who won the first ABA championship, in 1967–68?

3. Who won the last ABA title, in 1975–76?

4. During the nine years of the ABA's existence, only two teams won more than one title. Which two teams?

5. One of these two took three ABA championships. Which team?

6. The NBA record for the most points scored by one team in a single game is 173. But an ABA team scored 177 points in a single game, on April 12, 1970. Name this team.

7. The NBA record for the most points scored by two teams in a single game is 316. But two ABA teams scored 342 points on February 14, 1975. Which two teams?

8. The NBA's rival leagues had franchise names as colorful as we see today with the Utah Jazz, the San Antonio Spurs, or the Portland Trail Blazers. Abe Saperstein's short-lived ABL had, for example, the Chicago Majors, the Kansas City Steers, and the Hawaii Chiefs. The ABA had its own share of unusual team names— the San Diego Sails and the Virginia Hawks, to mention two. One southern city had an ABA team with three different names—the Pros, the Sounds, and the Tams. What city?

9. One team, the Claws, never even got to play, but was disbanded before its first season. What city did the Claws represent?

10. Pittsburgh began its ABA career in 1967–68 with one name and ended its five-year life in 1971–72 with another name. Someone said about the Pittsburgh team and its second name: "I don't know if they picked [this second name] because they're birds of prey or because they're about to become extinct." What was that second name?

THE NBA

11. The unquestioned kings of pro basketball were the Boston Celtics. Beginning in 1956–57, the Celtics won far more NBA championships than did any other team. How many championship flags are now flying in the Boston Garden?

12. Of these, how many did the Celtics win in a row? And what years did these consecutive titles cover?

13. Despite their seeming invincibility, none of the Boston Celtic teams of that period is considered the greatest NBA team of all time. That honor goes to another team of 1966–67. The selection was made by the NBA during its thirty-fifth anniversary celebration in October 1980. What team was picked as the single best team of all time?

14. Since the NBA's first season in 1946–47, only two teams—the Minneapolis Lakers and the Boston Celtics—have won consecutive championships. How many other teams have *repeated* as NBA champs?

15. If the NBA gave an award for frustration, it would surely go to the Los Angeles Lakers. They made the championship finals more times than any other team before they finally won their first title, in 1971–72. How many times before 1971–72 did Los Angeles make it to the finals?

16. In a five-year period, 1975 through 1980, five separate teams won the NBA title. One of these was Boston, 1975–76. Who were the other four?

17. Which team holds the record for the most games won in a single season? How many games, and what year?

18. This same team holds the record for the longest winning streak, established in the same season. How many games in a row did this team win?

19. Which team holds the record for the most games lost in a single season? How many games, and what year?

20. This same team held a previous record for the longest losing streak, established in that same season. How many games in a row did this team lose?

21. That record was recently broken by another team. Name it, and give the number of consecutive losses it had.

ANSWERS

THE ABA

1. *(A-b)* Anaheim Amigos
   (B-d) Dallas Chaparrals
   (C-j) Denver Rockets
   (D-f) Houston Mavericks
   (E-e) Kentucky Colonels
   (F-g) Minnesota Muskies
   (G-a) New Jersey Americans
   (H-c) New Orleans Buccaneers
   (I-h) Oakland Oaks
   (J-i) Pittsburgh Pipers

2. The Pittsburgh Pipers.

3. The New York Nets.

4. The Indiana Pacers and the New York Nets.

5. The Indiana Pacers, in 1969–70, 1971–72, and 1972–73. The New York Nets won their two ABA titles in 1973–74 and 1975–76.

6. Indiana scored 177 points on April 12, 1970, in a game against Pittsburgh. Bear in mind that the ABA had a three-point field goal, which the NBA did not authorize until the 1979–80 season.

7. On February 14, 1975, San Antonio scored 176 points against New York's 166, for a total of 342 points—many more than the NBA record of 316. But the ABA San Antonio-New York total included four overtimes and the three-point field goal.

8. Memphis, Tennessee.

9. Baltimore, Maryland.

10. *The Condors.*

THE NBA

11. *Fourteen. Boston won its 14th title in 1981.*

12. *Eight, 1958–59 through 1965–66.*

13. *The Philadelphia 76ers of 1966–67, with Wilt Chamberlain, Billy Cunningham, Hal Greer, Luke Jackson, Wali Jones, and Chet Walker. Combined, these six had the awesome total of 8,832 points for that season.*

14. *Aside from Minneapolis and Boston, only three cities have won more than one NBA championship—Philadelphia in 1946–47, 1955–56, and 1966–67, New York in 1969–70 and 1972–73, and Los Angeles in 1971–72 and 1979–80. Actually, Philadelphia represented two separate franchises; its first two NBA titles were won by the Philadelphia Warriors. When Philadelphia won its third title, it had a new franchise, the 76ers. The Warriors had moved to California.*

15. *Seven.*

16. *The other four teams were the Portland Trail Blazers, 1976–77; the Washington Bullets, 1977–78; the Seattle Super-Sonics, 1978–79; and the Los Angeles Lakers, 1979–80.*

17. *The Los Angeles Lakers won 69 games in 1971–72.*

18. *The Lakers won 33 games in a row during that same season—November 5, 1971 to January 7, 1972.*

19. *The Philadelphia 76ers lost 73 games in 1972–73, while winning only 9 games, for the worst record so far. Such a record would be expected from an expansion team, but the 76ers had been in the league for some time and had won the championship only six years before.*

20. *The 76ers also had the dubious distinction of having the longest losing streak in NBA history. That unhappy record was set in the same season of 1972–73, when the 76ers lost 20 games in a row.*

21. *Fortunately for the 76ers, this record was recently wiped out when the Detroit Pistons lost a total of 21 games in a row, covering the end of the 1979–80 season and the beginning of the 1980–81 season.*

Second Time out: ABA/NBA Stats, Etc.

1. The first commissioner of the ABA and the last were both former stars of the NBA. Name them.

2. Only one ABA player was named Rookie of the Year and Most Valuable Player in the same season, 1969–70. Who was he?

3. One ABA player received three awards as MVP, the only ABA player ever to do so. Name him. He is now an NBA superstar.

4. Connie Hawkins was 27 years old when he finally made it to the NBA, which had earlier refused to sign him. He played two seasons with the ABA; he was named the ABA's first MVP, and he won the ABA's first scoring title in 1967–68, with a 26.8 average. He jumped to the NBA in 1969–70, when he signed with the Phoenix Suns. Why did the NBA originally refuse to sign him, and why did they allow him to be signed in 1969?

5. The ABA lured coaches as well as players away from the NBA. Two of the better known coaches were Alex Hannum of the 76ers, who went to the ABA's Oakland Oaks, and Bill Sharman of the Golden State Warriors, who signed with the ABA's Los Angeles Stars. But the most famous ABA acquisition was Wilt Chamberlain, when he left the Los Angeles Lakers in 1973 to sign with an ABA team as a player-coach. What ABA team?

6. Among the all-time ABA scorers you will find such familiar names as Mel Daniels, Julius Erving, Spencer

Haywood, and Dan Issel. But there is one other player who has far more ABA records, including most career points scored, most assists, and most minutes played. Who is he? He played in the ABA for the Kentucky Colonels, in the NBA for the San Antonio Spurs.

7. He has two ABA records that may prove hard to match by NBA players. What two records?

8. Red Auerbach and Red Holzman are two of basketball's most famous coaches. What are their first names?

9. When Red Auerbach retired as a coach in 1966, he had won more games than any other coach in modern professional basketball. How many?

10. Five NBA coaches have won over 500 games. Red Auerbach leads the list, followed by Red Holzman. Name the other three.

11. Many players have become topnotch coaches, and many have functioned as player-coaches. Which of the following was *not* a player-coach? Al Attles, Bob Cousy, Dave Cowens, Dave DeBusschere, Bill Russell, Paul Silas, Jerry West, and Lenny Wilkens.

12. At least three-dozen players have scored 15,000 or more career points, and eleven have scored over 20,000. But only five have so far scored 25,000 or more career points. Name these five.

13. Which one of these five is the only player to score more than 30,000 career points?

14. Three of these five are the only players in NBA history to score 10,000 or more field goals. Who are they?

15. When we speak of "iron men" in sports, we immediately think of Lou Gehrig and his 2,130 consecutive baseball games. Basketball has its own iron men. One player appeared in 844 consecutive games, over a period of eleven seasons, until an injury in November,

1965, finally ended his streak. Name this iron man of basketball.

16. Another iron man never fouled out of a single game in his entire career, covering fourteen seasons and 1,045 games. In one season, 1961–62, he played a total of 3,882 minutes, or an average of 48.5 minutes per game (including overtimes) for every game of the 80-game season. Name *this* iron man.

17. The NBA recently selected its all-time All-NBA team. But there are many other great players besides the eleven chosen for that team. Here are eleven other players who have scored more than 15,000 career points. Match them with their teams. (Some of them played for more than one franchise.)

(A) Dick Barnett   (a) Atlanta-New Orleans-Boston

(B) Walt Bellamy   (b) Boston

(C) Dave Bing   (c) Chicago-Baltimore-New York-Atlanta

(D) Gail Goodrich   (d) Detroit

(E) Hal Greer   (e) Detroit

(F) Bailey Howell   (f) Detroit-Baltimore-Boston

(G) Lou Hudson   (g) Los Angeles

(H) Sam Jones   (h) Los Angeles-New York

(I) Bob Lanier   (i) New York-Phoenix

(J) Pete Maravich   (j) Philadelphia

(K) Dick Van Arsdale   (k) St. Louis-Atlanta-Los Angeles

ANSWERS

1. *George Mikan and Dave DeBusschere.*

2. *Spencer Haywood of the Denver Rockets.*

3. *Julius Erving of the New York Nets, in 1973–74, 1974–75, and 1975–76. He shared his second award with George McGinnis of the Indiana Pacers.*

4. *In the basketball scandal of 1961, Connie Hawkins was accused of having an association with Jack Molinas as an intermediary for Molinas and another convicted gambler. Hawkins had met Molinas, but he had never been bribed by Molinas or asked to fix games, which would have been impossible for him in any event, since he was only a college freshman and not eligible for varsity play. But the mention of Hawkins' name during the 1961 scandal was enough to bar him from the NBA. He did play pro ball with Abe Saperstein's ABL (he dropped out of college after his freshman year), spent four years with the Globetrotters and two years with the ABA, which did not have the same policy of barring players. Hawkins sued the NBA for excluding him from their league, and won a million-dollar settlement, including a long-term contract with the Phoenix Suns, in 1969. He retired from active playing in 1976, after seven successful seasons in the NBA, with a career total of 11,528 points. This total does not include his season and a half with the ABL and his four years with the Globetrotters.*

5. *The San Diego Conquistadores.*

6. *Louie Dampier. In nine ABA seasons, he had 13,726 points, 4,084 assists, and 27,770 minutes played.*

7. *Most 3-point field goals attempted, 2,217; and most 3-point field goals made, 794.*

8. Auerbach's first name is Arnold. Holzman's first name is William.

9. Auerbach has 938 pro victories. Including his wins as a high-school coach, he has over 1,000 victories, the only coach in modern basketball history to go over that mark.

10. Dick Motta, now with the Dallas Mavericks; Jack Ramsay of the Portland Trail Blazers; and Gene Shue, now coaching the San Diego Clippers.

11. Jerry West. He retired as an active player in 1974, and became coach of the Los Angeles Lakers two years later.

12. Kareem Abdul-Jabbar, Wilt Chamberlain, John Havlicek, Oscar Robertson, and Jerry West. (Rick Barry also has over 25,000 points, including his four seasons in the ABA. But the NBA does not recognize ABA scoring for its statistics.)

13. Wilt Chamberlain.

14. Kareem Abdul-Jabbar, Wilt Chamberlain, and John Havlicek.

15. John Kerr of the Syracuse Nationals and Philadelphia 76ers (Syracuse moved to Philadelphia in 1963 and changed its name to the 76ers), and the Baltimore Bullets. Kerr's streak began in 1954 and ended, finally, on November 5, 1965.

16. Wilt Chamberlain.

17. (A-h) Dick Barnett, Los Angeles-New York
    (B-c) Walt Bellamy, Chicago-Baltimore-New York-Atlanta
    (C-d) Dave Bing, Detroit-Washington
    (D-g) Gail Goodrich, Los Angeles-New Orleans
    (E-j) Hal Greer, Philadelphia
    (F-f) Bailey Howell, Detroit-Baltimore-Boston
    (G-k) Lou Hudson, St. Louis-Atlanta-Los Angeles
    (H-b) Sam Jones, Boston
    (I-e) Bob Lanier, Detroit
    (J-a) Pete Maravich, Atlanta-New Orleans-Boston
    (K-i) Dick Van Arsdale, New York-Phoenix

Play Resumes: The All-Time All-Stars

On October 30, 1980, as part of its thirty-fifth anniversary celebration, the NBA announced the names of eleven players who had been selected by a poll of the Professional Basketball Writers Association of America as the all-time NBA team. Of the eleven, eight are in the Basketball Hall of Fame; one has not been retired long enough for that honor, but will surely be included when he becomes eligible; and two, Kareem Abdul-Jabbar and Julius Erving, are still actively playing. These are the eleven (listed alphabetically):

Kareem Abdul-Jabbar, Elgin Baylor, Wilt Chamberlain, Bob Cousy, Julius Erving, John Havlicek, George Mikan, Bob Pettit, Oscar Robertson, Bill Russell, and Jerry West.

The same poll named Bill Russell as the greatest player of all time, Red Auerbach of the Celtics as the greatest coach, and the Philadelphia 76ers of 1966–67 as the single greatest team.

[145]

BOB COUSY

1. His playing career, both in college and the pros, was centered in New England—specifically, the Boston area. What college did he attend?

2. When he graduated, it was assumed he would be drafted by the Celtics. Much to the horror of the Boston fans, the Celtics passed him by and allowed him to go elsewhere. Yet he never did play for any other team (except for a brief time after his formal retirement). How did he end up with the Celtics?

3. Although Boston sportswriters and Boston fans clamored for Cousy to be drafted by the Celtics, Red Auerbach was originally convinced that the 6-foot 1-inch Cousy did not have the kind of talent he wanted on his team. Auerbach did not endear himself to Boston when he dismissed the newly graduated Cousy with a none-too-flattering phrase. What did Auerbach say about Cousy?

4. As the Lakers had their Elgin Baylor-Jerry West combination, so, too, did the Celtics have an outstanding backcourt duo. One-half of this combo was Bob Cousy. Who was the other half?

5. Cousy doesn't hold any current NBA scoring records, but he does have a record for consecutive appearances in All-Star games. How many?

6. Cousy had superb reflexes. He was an extraordinary ballhandler and passer, with a peripheral vision that seemed to give him a clear 180 degree view of the action on the court. He delighted fans everywhere with a passing maneuver he made famous. What was it? It's frequently used today.

7. In addition to the 14 championship banners the Boston Garden is now flying, it also has the retired numbers of its most famous players, including Bob Cousy's. What was his uniform number?

8. Six years after his retirement in 1963, he became coach of an NBA team. He coached this team for four-and-a-half seasons. In his first season as a coach, he actually put himself into seven games, but scored a total of only five points, and soon gave up the idea of coaching and playing at the same time. What team was it?

9. What's he doing now?

ANSWERS

1. *Holy Cross College, Worcester, Massachusetts.*

2. *He was drafted in 1950 by the Tri-Cities Blackhawks. Tri-Cities immediately traded him to the Chicago Stags, but the Stags folded shortly before the season opened. The names of three of the Chicago players were placed in a hat to be drawn by New York, Philadelphia, and Boston. New York and Philadelphia picked first and second, and were happy with their picks. The player that was left, Bob Cousy, went to Boston. Both Red Auerbach and Walter Brown, president of the Celtics, were convinced they had gotten the worst of the deal. (As a result of these various transactions, Cousy actually was a member of three separate teams without playing a minute of pro basketball.)*

3. *He called Cousy "a local yokel."*

4. *Bill Sharman.*

5. *Thirteen, one for each of his thirteen seasons with the Celtics. He was named MVP of the All-Stars twice, in 1954 and 1957.*

6. *A pass behind his back.*

7. *Number 14.*

8. *The Cincinnati Royals*

9. *He's a TV color commentator for the Boston Celtics.*

KAREEM ABDUL-JABBAR

1. When Kareem Abdul-Jabbar was still Lew Alcindor, he was one of the most sought-after high-school players in the country. Where did he go to high school?

2. As the star centerpiece for John Wooden's UCLA Bruins for three seasons—1966–67, 1967–68, and 1968–69—Lew Alcindor was a three-time All-American. How many times was he named the NCAA tournament's MVP?

3. He was drafted by the Milwaukee Bucks in 1969, but the Bucks actually won the right to sign him in a coin toss. Which was the club that lost out in that coin toss?

4. The date March 22 has a particular significance for him, specifically in 1969 and 1972. Explain.

5. How many NBA scoring titles has he won?

6. How many times has he been named the NBA's MVP?

7. During his first 10 years as a pro, how many times was he named to the annual all-NBA team?

8. An incident in the first game of the 1977–78 season is one he would just as soon forget. As a result of it, he suffered a broken wrist that sidelined him for 20 games. What was that incident?

9. He has a passion for collecting—what? He has over 3,000 of them.

ANSWERS

1. New York City, Power Memorial High School.

2. Three times.

3. The Phoenix Suns.

4. On March 22, 1969, Lew Alcindor was named the Most Valuable Player in that year's NCAA tournament, to become the first player to win that tournament's MVP award for three years in a row. Exactly three years later, on March 22, 1972, he was named the NBA's MVP for that season.

5. Two. He won his first scoring title as Lew Alcindor, in 1970–71, and his second scoring title a year later, after he had changed his name to Kareem Abdul-Jabbar.

6. He was named MVP a record six times: in 1970–71 (when he was still Lew Alcindor), 1971–72, 1973–74, 1975–76, 1976–77, and 1979–80.

7. Nine times, either to the first or second all-NBA teams. He missed only once, in 1974–75, when he was unhappy in Milwaukee, and unhappy with Larry Costello, the Bucks' coach. At the expiration of his contract, he was traded to the Los Angeles Lakers.

8. In the first game of the 1977–78 season, he got into a fight with his 6-foot 11-inch counterpart on the Milwaukee Bucks, rookie Kent Benson. Like many another hotshot rookie before him, Benson thought he could intimidate the famous Abdul-Jabbar with an elbow to the midsection. Abdul-Jabbar countered with a hefty right to the chin, and down went the 245-pound rookie with a broken jaw. Although it may have seemed that Benson got the worst of it, it was Abdul-Jabbar who suffered the most. In addition to a fractured wrist that lost him 20 games, he was slapped with a record $5,000 fine. By the time he returned to the lineup, he was fed up with pro basketball and threatened to quit the game. But a long talk with his coach, Jerry West, changed his mind. After that, he came on stronger than ever and ended the season with 1,609 points and a 25.8 average, enough to place him fourth among the top scorers.

9. *Jazz albums.*

JOHN HAVLICEK

1. He was born and raised in Lansing, Ohio, a town of three- or four-hundred people. He was a star high-school athlete, and was named Ohio all-state in two separate sports, football and basketball. When he graduated from high school, he was offered a football scholarship by one of the top teams in the nation. Who was the famous college football coach who wanted him as a passer?

2. Havlicek accepted a basketball scholarship at Ohio State, where he starred for four years, both on the freshman and varsity basketball teams. But he was again considered for football upon his graduation from college. He was drafted in 1962 by a team in the National Football League. What team?

3. Two pro basketball teams wanted him at the same time. One was Boston; the other was an ABL team that offered him $25,000—$10,000 more than the Celtics had offered. Name this ABL team.

4. He turned down both basketball offers and went, instead, to the NFL, where he appeared in one preseason exhibition football game, in 1962, against the Steelers. What position did he play?

5. He was cut from the NFL team after that one game, and that was enough pro football for Havlicek. He reported to the Celtics' rookie team, and spent his entire basketball career, 16 seasons, with Boston. What position did

he play for the Celtics? (Even though the ABL offer was much higher, he was skeptical about Saperstein's league, and preferred the NBA.)

6. Because of a certain ability he had, he fit perfectly into the Celtics' fast break and helped to make Boston's offense nearly unbeatable. What was this ability of his?

7. He is one of the five top NBA scorers of all time, but he holds no NBA scoring records. He does have two NBA records that may never be equaled. What are they?

8. How many NBA championship rings does he have?

9. When he retired in 1978, his number was retired with him. what was his uniform number?

ANSWERS

1. *Woody Hayes of Ohio State.*

2. *The Cleveland Browns.*

3. *The ABL's Cleveland Pipers.*

4. *He was drafted by the Browns as a quarterback but he was changed to a wide receiver when it was seen how well he could catch passes. Apparently he couldn't catch them that well, because he was cut after his one and only pro-football game.*

5. *He played both guard and forward, as the Celtics' famous "sixth man," coming in off the bench whenever Coach Auerbach needed a fresh player on offense. After four years as the sixth man, Havlicek moved into the starting lineup as a forward. Only 6 feet 5 inches, he proved that forwards did not have to be 6 feet 8 inches or over.*

6. *His ability to "run and run and run," after everyone else gave up or gave out. He later said that this ability of his had started in high school. "I was always able to run," he said. "In college I never got tired."*

7. *The most games played—1,270—and most minutes played—46,471.*

8. *Eight.*

9. *Number 17.*

ELGIN BAYLOR

1. When Baylor signed his first pro contract after graduation from Seattle University, the owner of Baylor's new club had this to say: "If he had turned me down, I'd have been out of business. The club would have been bankrupt." What faltering franchise did Baylor single-handedly save from extinction?

2. He scored a career total of 23,149 points, placing him in a select group. How many times did he win the NBA scoring title?

3. He was never named MVP, but he did win one other prestigious NBA award. What was it?

4. As a 6-foot 5-inch forward, he teamed with another all-time great to form what is generally conceded to be the best two-man scoring combination in NBA history. Who was the other half?

5. How many points per season did they average between them?

6. In his second season as a pro, Baylor scored a record-breaking 64 points in one game, erasing a previous record. He broke his own record a year later. How many points did he score in his second record-breaking performance?

7. In his 14 years as a pro, how many times was he one of the league's five top scorers?

8. He had a brief career as a coach. With what NBA team?

ANSWERS

1. *The Minneapolis Lakers. The Lakers moved to Los Angeles in 1960–61. Baylor spent his entire playing career, 1958 through 1972, with the Lakers.*

2. *He never won an NBA scoring title.*

3. *Rookie of the Year, 1958–59.*

4. *Baylor teamed with fellow-Laker Jerry West as one of the most potent one-two combos of all time.*

5. *During their 10 most productive seasons together, they scored a total of 38,351 points for a per-season average of 3,835 points.*

6. *On November 15, 1960, Baylor scored 71 points against the New York Knicks–a new record for points scored in a single game by an individual. Unfortunately, this record lasted only 16 months.*

7. *Seven times*

8. *The New Orleans Jazz. In two and a half seasons as coach of the Jazz, Baylor won 86 games and lost 134.*

WILT CHAMBERLAIN

1. He is listed as having played for three separate franchises in three separate cities. But one city was actually two different franchises. Name the city and the two different clubs he played for in that city.

2. He has a bushelful of NBA scoring records, more than any other man, but he doesn't own *all* scoring records. Which of the following does he not have? Most field goals attempted, most field goals made, most free throws attempted, and most free throws made.

3. His unequaled string of scoring titles began in his rookie year, 1959–60, when he had 2,707 points and a 37.6 average for a new season high. How many consecutive scoring titles did he win?

4. It was his third season, 1961–62, that saw him reach unparalleled heights. He had 4,029 points, and averaged a phenomenal 50.4 points a game. He scored 60 or more points 15 times, and 50 or more points 44 times. Never before and never again has anyone matched those totals. But it was one spectacular game in that season, played on March 2, 1962, that most fans remember as Chamberlain's single greatest feat. What was it?

5. Darrall Imhoff and Dave Budd share that feat with him. Why?

6. How many times was Chamberlain named MVP?

7. How many NBA championship rings does he have?

8. How tall is he?

9. Who said this about playing against Chamberlain? "I have a three-part defense I use against him. One, I try to keep him from the ball. Two, if that doesn't work, I try to stay between him and the basket. Three is when everything else fails: I panic."

10. Among his other passions, Chamberlain loves cars, and owns two of the finest. Which ones?

ANSWERS

1. *The Philadelphia Warriors and the Philadelphia 76ers. Chamberlain began his NBA career with the Philadelphia Warriors in 1959–60, after a year with the Globetrotters. When the team moved to San Francisco in 1962 to become the San Francisco Warriors, he moved with them. In 1965 he returned to Philadelphia to play for the 76ers. In one of the most stunning trades of all time, Chamberlain went to the Los Angeles Lakers in 1968, and played out his last five seasons with the Lakers.*

2. *Most field goals attempted, and most free throws made. He holds the record for most free throws attempted—11,862—but did not make all that many. By his own admission, he wasn't too expert at the free-throw line.*

3. *Seven. From his rookie year, 1959–60, through 1965–66. He never again won a scoring title.*

4. *He scored 100 points, against the Knicks, the first and only time any pro player had scored that total in a single game. He wiped out Elgin Baylor's 71-point record, set in the previous season.*

5. *Darall Imhoff and Dave Budd were the unfortunate Knick centers who had to guard Chamberlain on that momentous night of March 2, 1962. Darall Imhoff played against Chamberlain for 20 minutes, and Dave Budd for 27 minutes. Although Imhoff and Budd scored only 20 points between them, the Knicks as a team pumped in 147, good enough to win almost any game. But this wasn't "almost any game." It was Wilt's greatest. Sadly for the Knicks, Wilt and the Warriors scored a total of 169 points, which helped to set another NBA record—most points scored by both teams in a single game, 316.*

6. *Four times—the first time in his rookie year, and then three seasons in a row, 1965–66 through 1967–68.*

7. *Two. He won his first champsionship ring with the 76ers of 1966–67 and his second with the Los Angeles Lakers of 1971–72.*

8. *Exactly 7 feet and 1-1/16th inch—lying down.*

9. *Bill Russell.*

10. *A Bentley and a Maserati.*

JULIUS ERVING

1. He was a star in high school, but actually honed his early skills on a hometown playground. There is a sign on that playground that reads: "This is where Julius Erving learned the game of basketball." Name his hometown.

2. He spent three years at the University of Massachusetts, and left after his juinor year to sign a four-year, $500,000 contract with an ABA team. What team?

3. One year later, an NBA team drafted him. Name that team, and explain why it drafted him even though he was already playing in the ABA.

4. Erving functioned briefly as a coach-player in the 1972–73 season. In how many games? And what is his record as a coach?

5. At the end of that season he was sold to the New York Nets for $1,000,000 and one player. With Erving on their roster, the Nets enjoyed the three finest seasons of their existence: they won their first ABA title in 1973–74, finished in a tie for first place in the Eastern Division in 1974–75 (they were eliminated in the first round of the playoffs), and once again won the ABA title in 1975–76. Most of their success was attributed to Erving. Yet the Nets sold him to the 76ers. Why?

6. He won the ABA's MVP award three times. How many ABA scoring titles did he win?

7. How many NBA scoring titles has he won?

8. He is a dazzling playmaker who sometimes seems to walk on air as he leaps toward the basket and makes an impossible twist to avoid a defender and manages, somehow, to sink his shot with a backward flip of his arm. He is a master of the dunk, although he once stuffed the ball so hard he injured his right wrist. What position does he play, and how tall is he?

9. On May 27, 1981, he was named the NBA's Most Valuable Player for the 1980–81 season. Aside from the fact that this was his first MVP award in the NBA, what else was unusual about it?

ANSWERS

1. *Roosevelt, Long Island, New York.*

2. *The Virginia Squires.*

3. *Erving was drafted by the NBA's Milwaukee Bucks on April 10, 1972, even though he had already played one year of pro basketball for the ABA's Virginia Squires. The NBA considered him eligible for drafting because his class at the University of Massachusetts graduated in the spring of 1972, when he would have been available for drafting if he had not left college the year before. And the NBA, in the midst of its bidding war with the ABA, was using every tactic it could to draw prospects away from its rival. The courts, however, ruled that Erving had to honor his contract with the ABA Squires.*

4. *In the final game of the 1972–73 season, Al Bianchi, coach of the Squires, left to scout the Kentucky Colonels, whom the Squires would be facing in the first round of the ABA playoffs. He put Erving in charge of the Squires' last regular-season game. The Squires beat the New York Nets, 121–106, and thus gave Erving a perfect record of 1–0 as a coach.*

5. *When the New York Nets were absorbed into the NBA at the close of the 1975–76 season, Roy Boe, owner of the Nets, had to pay the NBA an entry fee of $3,200,000. The price was so steep, Boe had to cut corners somewhere. He figured the best place to start was with his most expensive player, Julius Erving, so he traded away the Nets' only genuine superstar to the 76ers. As a result of that sale, the Nets went into a decline from which they have not yet recovered.*

6. *Three, in 1972–73, 1973–74, and 1975–76. He missed making it four in a row when he lost the 1974–75 title by a bare 20 points. In that year he scored 2,343 points to George McGinnis 2,363.*

7. *He has never won an NBA scoring title.*

8. *He is a 6-foot 6-inch forward.*

9. *He was the first player not a center to win the award in 17 years.*

GEORGE MIKAN

1. As Wilt Chamberlain, Bill Russell, and Kareem Abdul-Jabbar dominated later basketball, so, too, did George Mikan dominate basketball in his time. He was All-American for three straight years while starring for DePaul University. He won another collegiate honor for two straight years, 1945 and 1946. What honor?

2. At 6 feet 10 inches, the bespectacled Mikan was the most widely publicized college star of the 1940s. When he graduated, he turned pro, playing for a team in the National Basketball League. Many NBL teams had industrial businesses as sponsors. Who sponsored Mikan's team?

3. He went from the NBL into the new NBA, to play for that league's Minneapolis Lakers. He led the Lakers to five NBA championships, and he set many records How many times did he win the NBA scoring title?

4. Out of his six complete seasons in the NBA, how many times did he lead the selections for the All-NBA teams?

5. Although all of his records have since been erased by more recent players, he has one award that can never be surpassed, but can be equaled. What award?

6. A distinction of another kind was given to him one night by Madison Square Garden. What was it? No, it was not a special "George Mikan Night."

7. He had an unusual uniform number, once seen, you would never forget. What number?

8. Mikan's 6 feet 10 inches and 245 pounds made him an ideal target for the opposition. During his playing career he suffered many broken bones—each leg once, the arch of his left foot, his right wrist, his nose, and one thumb. It was no wonder that he announced his retirement in 1954, when he was only 30. The basketball community was stunned by his announcement, but one person who stood to lose the most made this philosophical comment: "This should even up our league." Who said that?

9. What is Mikan doing now?

ANSWERS

1. *He was Player of the Year in 1945 and 1946.*

2. *Mikan's first pro team was the "American Gears," sponsored by the American Gear Company of Chicago.*

3. *Three times, all in succession, from 1948–49 through 1950–51.*

4. *He made the All-NBA team for each of his six complete seasons, and led the list for the first five years.*

5. *On February 15, 1950, a nationwide poll conducted by the Associated Press among sportswriters and sportscasters chose the top athletes of the twentieth century's first 50 years. The winners included such outstanding sports figures as Babe Ruth, Jack Dempsey, Bobby Jones, Bill Tilden, and Johnny Weismuller—and George Mikan as the top basketball player of the first half-century.*

6. *For one particular game, with the Minneapolis Lakers as the visitors, Madison Square Garden had a simple message on its marquee: "Tonite, George Mikan vs. Knicks."*

7. *Ninety-nine.*

8. *Johnny Kundla, the Lakers' coach.*

9. *Mikan is a lawyer.*

BOB PETTIT

1. He brought impressive credentials with him when he was drafted into the NBA in 1954. A consensus All-American in that season, he averaged 27.4 points a game for his three collegiate varsity years. What NBA team drafted him?

2. Critics said he was too skinny—at 6 feet 9 inches and 215 pounds—for professional basketball. But he quickly proved his right to be in the NBA by scoring 1,466 points in his rookie year to rank fourth among the NBA's top scorers. How many NBA scoring titles did he win after that?

3. How many times was he named MVP?

4. He had a long string of successive appearances in All-Star games. How many?

5. He holds the record for MVP awards in All-Star games. How many such awards did he win?

6. Early in his pro career, his team, the St. Louis Hawks, made a publicity tour of Mexico. In Mexico City there were life-sized posters of Pettit all over the city, with a caption that seemed to refute the Associated Press honor that had been given to George Mikan a couple of years before. What was that caption? It was printed in Spanish.

7. One of the NBA's more memorable performances came in the sixth and final game of the 1958 championship series, when the St. Louis Hawks defeated the Boston

Celtics for the NBA title. Pettit scored 50 points in that game, which saw the Celtics go down to defeat 110–108. Red Auerbach commented, half-jestingly that if the player guarding Pettit had kept Pettit to 48 points, the Celtics would have won the title. Who was that famous Celtic forward who permitted Pettit to score his 50 points?

8. Another game Pettit remembers with fondness took place on a Friday the thirteenth in November, 1964. Either Pettit wasn't superstitious, or the Friday the thirteenth jinx didn't work that night. What happened in that game?

9. What is Pettit doing now?

ANSWERS

1. *The Milwaukee Hawks.*

2. *One, in 1955–56.*

3. *Twice, in 1955–56 and again in 1958–59.*

4. *Eleven.*

5. *Four.*

6. *El mas grande jugador del basketbol del mundo–"The greatest basketball player in the world."*

7. *Tom Heinsohn.*

8. *He scored 29 points to become the first player in NBA history to go over 20,000 career points. His 29 points that evening gave him a total of 20,022. He retired at the end of that 1964–65 season with a career total of 20,880 points, the highest in NBA history to that point. But this record lasted less than a year. On February 14, 1966, Wilt Chamberlain scored his 20,884th point.*

9. *Pettit is a banker, and freely admits that he "looks like one."*

OSCAR ROBERTSON

1. During his collegiate career, he was hailed as "quite possibly the greatest player in the history of college basketball." By the time he graduated from the University of Cincinnati in 1960, he held 14 NCAA records. He also won three separate prestigious awards for each of his three varsity seasons. Name these awards.

2. In his sophomore year he dazzled Madison Square Garden with an awesome display of shooting when he single-handedly beat the opposing team by scoring 56 points, more points than *all of his opponents combined*. Who were Cincinnati's unhappy victims that evening? The final score was 118–54.

3. Robertson was not just a basketball jock. As a high-school student, he graduated in the upper tenth of his class and was elected to the National Honor Society. In college he had one other distinction that set him apart from his University of Cincinnati teammates. What was it?

4. In 1960 he teamed with other future NBA superstars Walt Bellamy, Jerry Lucas, and Jerry West to play a series of eight games. What was the occasion, and how many of the eight did they win?

5. He was drafted by the Cincinnati Royals in 1960 and spent the first nine seasons of his career with them. He was traded in 1970, and played out his last four seasons with a second team. Name it.

6. How many of the following did he *not* win? Rookie of the Year, the NBA's Most Valuable Player, the All-Star games MVP, and the NBA scoring title.

7. How many NBA championship rings does he have?

8. How many consecutive times did he make the list of the NBA's top five scorers?

9. With a career total of 26,710 points (making him one of the five players to go over 25,000), he had a fabulous career. But he retired in 1974 with only two all-time NBA records. What are they?

ANSWERS

1. The national collegiate scoring title, consensus All-American, and Player of the Year.

2. Seton Hall.

3. He was the University of Cincinnati's first black basketball player.

4. They were all on the 1960 Olympic basketball team, generally regarded as the strongest ever to represent the United States in the Olympics. They swept their eight games—four of them by margins of more than 40 points—to take the gold medal.

5. The Milwaukee Bucks.

6. The NBA scoring title.

7. One, in 1970–71, when Milwaukee won its first and only NBA title.

8. Beginning with his rookie year, 1960–61, Robertson made the NBA's five top scorers for seven successive seasons.

9. Most assists, 9,887; and most free throws made, 7,694.

BILL RUSSELL

1. Although he was recently selected as the greatest player of all time, he was never recognized as a fantastic shooter. In his entire professional career he scored less than 15,000 points. But in 1955, his junior year at the University of San Francisco, he won a scoring title and an award to go with it. What were they?

2. He was drafted by the Celtics in 1956, but did not report for his pro debut until December 22, well into the season. Explain.

3. Not everyone shared Red Auerbach's high opinion of Russell's ability. Many fans were openly skeptical. "He can't shoot," they said, "he can't score, so what good is he?" But Auerbach knew why he wanted Russell. What Russell abililty was it that had so appealed to Auerbach?

4. Many basketball games are decided by the matchups—which player is assigned by his coach to go against a particular opponent. Bill Russell was half of the most famous matchups the NBA has ever seen. Who was his opponent in those matchups?

5. Russell has more NBA championship rings than any other player. How many?

6. How many times did he win the MVP award?

7. He never won an NBA scoring title, and, in fact, never placed among the NBA's five top scorers. But he made another important category of the top five for 12 of his 13 seasons with the Celtics. He was first in this category four times and second five times. What category of top five?

8. Russell spent his last three years with the Celtics as a player-coach. He retired as a player at the end of the 1968–69 season, and later coached another NBA team for four years. What was this second team he coached?

9. What was his overall record as a coach, including his three seasons as a player-coach?

10. His uniform number hangs in Boston Garden along with the retired numbers of other Celtic greats. What was Russell's number?

ANSWERS

1. *In the NCAA tournament of 1955, when San Francisco defeated LaSalle to take the NCAA title, Russell won the scoring honors with 118 points in five games. He was also named the tournament's MVP.*

2. *In the summer of 1956 he went to Melbourne, Australia, as part of the American Olympic team. After the Olympics, the victorious United States team appeared in other international tournaments, including that year's Gold Medal. Russell returned to the United States in mid-December. But he couldn't report to the Celtics quite yet. First of all, he married a young lady named Rose Swisher, and second, there was a short honeymoon. Honeymoon or no, Russell found time to sign his contract with the Celtics, for a figure somewhere between $19,000 and $24,000, making him the highest-paid rookie of his time.*

3. *His superb rebounding and his uncanny ability to block shots. In Auerbach's words: "Russell made shot-blocking an art."*

4. *Wilt Chamberlain.*

5. *Eleven.*

6. *Five, second only to Kareem Abdul-Jabbar's six.*

7. *The top rebounders. The five times he was second he was beaten out by Wilt Chamberlain.*

8. *The Seattle SuperSonics.*

9. *His overall record as a coach was 324 wins and 249 losses. With the Celtics, his teams won 162 games and lost 83. The SuperSonics did not do as well for him: while they won the same number, 162, they lost 166.*

10. *Number 6.*

JERRY WEST

1. In his senior high-school year, he was selected for the All-American high-school squad. Where did he attend high school?

2. As a collegiate player at West Virginia University, he did not win any scoring titles, but he won a top honor in his junior and senior years. What honor?

3. In his 14 seasons with the Los Angeles Lakers, he became one of the NBA's all-time superstars, but he did not have a spectacular rookie year. He averaged only 17.6 points per game in 1960–61, his first pro season, while his fellow rookie, Oscar Robertson, was averaging 30.5. West more than made up for it in subsequent seasons. How many NBA scoring titles did he eventually win?

4. One of his coaches said about West: "He is the man who has everything—a fine shooting touch, speed, quickness, all the physical assets, including a tremendous dedication to the game." The rest of the NBA agreed with him; West was consistently named to the All-NBA teams. How many times did he make either the first or second team?

5. He was never named the NBA's MVP, but he did win one award as an All-Star MVP. What year?

6. He had one unforgettable moment in the third game of the 1970 championship finals. What was it?

7. Despite his slight stature—6 foot 3 inches and 175

pounds—he willingly and aggressively mixed it up under the boards with his much bigger opponents. This apparent recklessness resulted in a recurring injury he suffered so often it had to be a record. What injury, and how many times did it happen?

8. The three great Laker superstars, now retired—Elgin Baylor, Wilt Chamberlain, and Jerry West—own most of the all-time Laker records. West has two of them. What are they?

9. He had the same uniform number both in college and with the Lakers. What number?

ANSWERS

1. *East Bank, West Virginia.*

2. *He was consensus All-American for two consecutive seasons, 1958–59 and 1959–60.*

3. *One, in 1969–70.*

4. *Twelve times. He made the All-NBA first team ten times, and the second team twice. He missed only in his rookie year, 1960–61, and in his final season, 1973–74.*

5. *1972.*

6. *The third game of the 1970 championship finals, between the Lakers and the Knicks, literally went down to the final buzzer. With three seconds left, Dave DeBusschere sank a 15-footer to give the Knicks a two point lead. Wilt Chamberlain took the ball out of bounds and threw it in to Jerry West, who dribbled twice, and let fly with a 61-footer. It went in just as the buzzer sounded, to tie the score and send the game into overtime. But the Lakers lost in overtime, 111–108, and eventually lost the championship to the Knicks, four games to three.*

7. *A broken nose, which he sustained eight times.*

8. *Most career points—25,192; and most career assists— 6,238.*

9. *Number 44.*

Last Time out

The score is tied, with only seconds left to play. The opposing benches are gathered around their respective coaches, who are feverishly explaining matchups or last-second plays to score or to get the ball back.

While all of this hurried activity is going on down on the floor, let's take another breather for a few more basketball anecdotes, both serious and amusing.

When Luther Gulick and James Naismith first began thinking of a new game for their students, they had in mind something nonviolent—not necessarily genteel, but certainly nothing as brutal or bonecrushing as basketball can be today. Some of the stories that follow show how rough the game has become, and how far it has traveled from the more gentlemanly sport of Naismith's time.

On the night of December 7, 1977, the Los Angeles Lakers and the Houston Rockets were playing in Los Angeles. Two 6-foot 8-inch forwards, one of them a Houston Rocket weighing 218 pounds, and the other a 230-pound Laker, were matched against each other. Suddenly, within full view of a horrified television audience, the Laker forward, Kermit Washington, threw a deadly punch that shattered the face of his Houston opponent, Rudy Tomjanovich.

Tomjanovich's face was almost completely destroyed, and he lost the rest of that season. Washington was given a 60-day suspension and fined $10,000. He received sacks of hate mail and death threats. The Lakers traded him to Boston, which traded him to San Diego, which traded him to Portland. Tomjanovich sued and won a $3.1-million award in the summer of 1979. The Rockets settled with the Lakers out-of-court for the loss of his services.

Both Washington and Tomjanovich have done their best since then to forget the incident. Washington has done a creditable job with Portland as one of the keys in their defense. Tomjanovich is once again playing with the Rockets, performing his specialty—a bank shot. At the end of the 1980–81 season he had 13,383 career points.

On the lighter side, there was an earlier incident involving two much bigger men—6-foot 9-inch, 235-pound Zelmo Beaty, who was then playing with the St. Louis Hawks (later to become the Atlanta Hawks), and 7-foot 1-inch, 275-pound Wilt Chamberlain, of the Philadelphia Warriors.

As Chamberlain tells the story, Beaty had a habit of standing on your toes when you tried to run or jump, or yanking at your shorts to slow you down. Beaty did that once too often to Chamberlain, who gave him what he calls "a gentle push back." Beaty went flying across the floor as if he'd been shot out of a cannon.

The referee ran over and told him not to get up. "Don't even twitch a muscle," the referee said. "Wilt's mad, and if he thinks you're already dead, he might not come over to look."

The Warriors were a tough bunch. Al Attles (now coaching the Golden State Warriors) was a terror in his own right. At 6 foot 2 inches and 175 pounds, he was not big enough to strike instant fear into the hearts of his opponents, but he was belligerent enough to have earned his nickname, "The Enforcer."

One overambitious rookie got *too* ambitious during an exhibition game; he kept hooking Attles, who warned him not to do it again. When the rookie ignored the warning, Attles flattened him with one punch. The referee jumped on the fallen rookie and whispered to him, "Kid, stay down. It may be the last time you get up."

Bob Pettit has his own story to tell. One night, during the 1957–58 season, he tried to break up a scrap between a fellow Hawk and a player from the Detroit Pistons. Someone hit him with a body block and knocked him from midcourt all the way to the scorer's table, which had curtains hanging over the front and the back. Pettit fell underneath, behind the curtains, where it was pitch black. When his head cleared, he peeked through the curtains, saw that the fight was still going on, and sat where he was until the police restored peace and quiet.

Basketball is not all macho male violence. There is emotion as well, sometimes deeply felt. Fred "Mad Dog" Carter, a 6-foot 3-inch guard with Baltimore, Philadelphia, and Milwaukee, spent eight seasons in the NBA until a severely sprained ankle in 1977 prematurely ended his playing days. He took a job coaching a women's team at his alma mater, tiny Mount St. Mary's College of Emmitsburg, Maryland.

In one of his first games, a Mount St. Mary's player fouled out. When she came to the bench, Carter thought he saw tears. "Is she crying?" he whispered to one of her teammates. "Yes," the young woman replied, "didn't you cry when you fouled out?"

The coach of a girls' high school team in Belmar, New Jersey, has his own view of basketball sexism: "We play a man-to-man defense," he said. "Person-to-person sounds like a phone call."

The commissioner of the NBA liked to think big. He predicted that within 10 years the NBA would be renamed the "International Basketball Association," with teams from Italy, Spain, Mexico, the Philippines, and Hawaii, among others.

Who made that prediction, and when did he make it? It was Walter Kennedy, who said that in March of 1971.

So far, the NBA has gotten no farther than Texas and California.

The "Big E," Elvin Hayes, unwittingly participated in what has to be a genuine first. His team, the San Diego Rockets (now the Houston Rockets), were in New York for a game with the Knicks. During the game, a fan came out of the stands at the Garden holding up a jersey with Hayes' old number from the University of Houston—number 44. Perhaps assuming the jersey was a copy, Hayes obligingly autographed it for the fan. Only later did he learn that it had actually been his own old jersey—stolen right off the back of an Elvin Hayes mannequin at the Basketball Hall of Fame.

Larry Bird may not yet be in Yogi Berra's class, but he may get there one day. When he was in the process of signing his extremely lucrative contract with the Celtics, he was given a tour of Boston by his agent, who asked him: "Is Boston better or worse than you thought it would be?"

Bird replied, "About the same."

On another occasion, Bird was asked how he thought he would do with the Celtics, who had fared badly the previous season.

"Very few people can turn a team around by themselves," he said, "and I'm not one of them."

OVERTIME

Famous Nicknames

Match the following nicknames to their respective players, and explain how the nicknames came about.

1. Houdini of the Hardwood.
2. The Big Dipper.
3. Dr. J.
4. Mr. K.
5. Dr. Dunk.
6. Hondo.
7. Clyde.
8. Dollar Bill.
9. Big Blue.
10. Secretary of the Defense.
11. The Twin Towers.

ANSWERS

1. Bob Cousy. Cousy's best-known nickname is "The Cooz." But sportswriters forever thought up new ones for him, usually having to do with his seemingly magical ballhandling skills. One nickname was "The Mobile Magician." Another one, even more descriptive, was "The Houdini of the Hardwood."

2. Wilt Chamberlain. He is perhaps better known by one of the most famous nicknames in all of sports—"Wilt the Stilt." But to his friends, to most sportswriters, and to knowledgeable basketball people, he is the "Big Dipper." As a growing boy, Chamberlain was called "Dip" by one of the kids in his neighborhood because he was so tall he had to dip under doorways. The name eventually evolved into "Dipper" and finally "The Big Dipper." This nickname led Chamberlain to christen both his boat and his million-dollar home "Ursa Major," the Latin name for the constellation.

3. "Dr. J" is of course the incomparable Julius Erving. As a youngster. Erving thought of becoming a doctor some day. In high school, one of his classmates called himself "The Professor." Not to be outdone, Julius Erving began calling himself "The Doctor." Teammate Willie Sojourner of the Virgina Squires later formalized it as "Doctor J," often written shorter as "Dr. J."

4. "Mr. K." is Larry Kenon, 6-foot 9-inch forward now with the San Antonio Spurs. Kenon played his college basketball at Memphis State University, where he was dubbed "Dr. K," after the fabulous Dr. J. When Kenon came into the pro ranks, he joined the New York Nets in 1973. Since the Nets already had a doctor—Dr. J himself—Dr. K was demoted to "Mr. K." Since then, sportswriters have tried other nicknames for Kenon—notably "Special K."

5. *"Dr. Dunk?"* Who else but the irrepressible Darryl Dawkins of the 76ers, who also likes to refer to himself as "Dr. Dunkenstein." His fellow Philadelphia athlete, Mike Schmidt of the Phillies, dubbed him "Sir Slam," after Dawkins broke two backboards with his enthusiastic dunk shots. Dawkins is not the only dunk specialist, but he seems to do it with more verve than anyone else. He has a "Dawkins Dunk-A-Log," which lists his most famous stuff shots—the Go-Rilla Dunk, the Look Out Below, the One We Owe You, the Spine Chiller Supreme, and the Dunk-You-Very-Much Dunk.

6. Just mention the name "Hondo" anywhere in Boston, and practially everyone—man, woman, or child—will know you're talking about John Havlicek. A fellow Ohioan and Ohio State teammate, Mel Nowell, could never quite pronounce Havlicek's name properly. He thought that Havlicek looked like John Wayne in profile, so he decided to call Havlicek "Hondo"—the name of a Wayne movie then being shown.

7. The nickname "Clyde," which belongs to Walt Frazier of the New York Knicks, also had its derivation in the movies. Frazier was always a snappy dresser, and showed a preference for the wide-brimmed hats and the 1930s style of dress seen in the movie Bonnie and Clyde. To his Knick teammates he became Clyde, and soon after, to the rest of the basketball community.

8. *"Dollar Bill?"* That's for another New York Knick, Bill Bradley, who was celebrated among his teammates for "the glint of [his] big initial contract," and for his frugality.

9. Bob Pettit had his own brand of thriftiness. When he was starring for the St. Louis Hawks, he wore an old blue overcoat. St. Louis broadcaster Buddy Blattner started calling him "Big Blue." Although the coat has long since been put away, the name stuck.

10. *"Secretary of the Defense?"* That can be only one man—Bill Russell, renowned for his ability to block shots.

11. *"The Twin Towers"* are Bill Cartwright and Marvin Webster of the New York Knicks, 7-feet 1-inch and 7-feet respectively. Their heights speak for themselves. When Knick coach Red Holzman puts both Cartwright and Webster on the floor at the same time, they are truly "Twin Towers."

DOUBLE OVERTIME

Who Said What, When, and Why

WHO SAID—

1. "When Oscar Robertson talks, you *listen!*"

2. "Think how I must feel. I'm the guy who didn't want [him]. What a genius!"

3. "Either I'm seeing double or there's ten of them out there!"

4. "'Close' only counts in horse shoes, hand grenades, and drive-in movies."

5. "Young man, you have the question backward."

6. "[He's] just like any other 7-foot black millionaire living next door to you."

7. "He's 7-2 and very gifted. I'm only 6-11½ and very gifted."

8. "It's easy, once you learn how to fly."

9. "I think that I shall never see a thing more lovely than a three."

10. "I'm a sub orchestra leader, and somehow they gave me the Philadelphia Orchestra to lead."

11. "It would be fun to play on the team. I'd make a hell of a guard."

ANSWERS

1. *Kareem Abdul-Jabbar. When he was still Lew Alcindor, he told an interviewer about some advice he had once received from Oscar Robertson. "What did you do?" the interviewer asked. Alcindor replied, "I listened, man, that's what I did! When Oscar Robertson talks, you listen!"*

2. *Walter Brown, president of the Boston Celtics, on the night of March 17, 1963, when Bob Cousy officially retired. The 43-minute pregame ceremony at the Boston Garden has been called "the most emotional sporting event" in Boston's history. In an effort to lighten the proceedings, Brown told the crowd: "Think how I must feel. I'm the guy who didn't want Cousy. What a genius!"*

3. *Hot Rod Hundley of the Los Angeles Lakers, as he returned to the bench one night during a game with the Boston Celtics. The Celtics were checking so well Hundley was convinced there had to be ten Celtics on the floor rather than the regulation five.*

4. *Bill Fitch, now coaching the Boston Celtics. He coached the Cleveland Cavaliers for nine seasons before signing with Boston. In 1970–71, when the Cavaliers were the new kids on the block, one of that season's three expansion teams, they won only 15 games. Fitch was kidded when the Cavs once came close to winning. He responded, "'Close' only counts in horse shoes, hand grenades, and drive-in movies."*

5. *Bill Russell, when asked how he would have fared against Kareem Abdul-Jabbar, answered, "Young man, you have the question backward."*

6. *Alex Hannum, who coached Wilt Chamberlain in San Francisco and Phildelphia. When he was asked what Wilt was* really like, he would answer, "Wilt is like any other 7-foot black millionaire living next door to you."

7. In 1974 when Bob Lanier was playing with the Detroit Pistons, he was told that a basketball expert had ranked Kareem Abdul-Jabbar as the number-one center in pro basketball, and Lanier number two. Lanier didn't agree that Abdul-Jabbar was better. "He's 7-2 and very gifted," Lanier said. "I'm only 6-11 1/2 and very gifted."

8. Julius Erving, when he was asked about his dunking ability. "It's easy," he said, "once you learn how to fly."

9. NBA Commissioner Lawrence O'Brien. In June 1979 the NBA discussed the 3-point field goal (which the ABA had successfully used). When the 3-point field goal was approved at a meeting of the NBA on Florida's Amelia Island, O'Brien said, "I think that I shall never see a thing more lovely than a three."

10. Paul Westhead, coach of the Los Angeles Lakers. In the 1979–80 season he was an assistant coach, with Jack McKinney as head coach. After a brief 13 games, McKinney fell from a bicycle and suffered head injuries severe enough to hospitalize him for many weeks. Assistant Paul Westhead led the team for the balance of that season, and was given a long-term contract, beginning with the 1980–81 season, to be the new head coach of the Lakers, replacing McKinney who had never returned after his accident. It was a promotion Westhead did not expect, and he said about his new responsibilities: "I'm a sub orchestra leader, and somehow they gave me the Philadelphia Orchestra to lead."

11. George Mikan. At 6-feet 10-inches he was one of the tallest centers of his time, but apparently he thought he wasn't all that tall. When he was asked his opinion of the NBA's thirty-fifth anniversary All-Time team, he said, "It would be fun to play on the team. I'd make a hell of a guard."

TRIPLE OVERTIME

NBA Odds and Ends

1. Who was the shortest player ever to win an NBA scoring title?

2. Who was the tallest player to win a scoring title?

3. Which of the following has *never* been named the NBA's MVP? Rick Barry, Walt Frazier, Richie Guerin, John Havlicek, Elvin Hayes, Jerry Lucas, Pete Maravich, Earl Monroe, Willis Reed, Nate Thurmond, and Chet Walker?

4. Not many athletes have the stamina or the skill to succeed in two pro sports at the same time. A 6-foot 8-inch center named Gene Conley did it in the late 1950s and the early 1960s when he played basketball for the Boston Celtics and baseball for the Phillies and the Red Sox. One famous New York Knick also played both pro basketball and pro baseball at the same time. Who was he?

5. In a game between the New Jersey Nets and the Philadelphia 76ers, three players played for *both teams*. How was that possible? No, they were not traded between halves.

6. Although Darryl Dawkins of the Philadelphia 76ers is a better-than-average player, he is probably better-known today for the backboards he shattered in late 1979 than for his basketball ability. But a player for the Baltimore Bullets predated Dawkins' feats by 16 years. In 1963 he shattered a backboard in Oakland, followed that two years later with another demolishing of a backboard in St. Louis, and did it for a third time in January 1971 in Milwaukee. Who was he?

7. The NBA has had two Rhodes scholars. Bill Bradley of the New York Knicks was one of them. Who is the other?

8. Almost without exception, the NBA uses only college graduates or college students. But there are currently two famous exceptions, neither one of whom went to college. Moses Malone is one. Name the other.

9. What do the following ten players have in common? Dave Bing, Dave Cowens, Julius Erving, Walt Frazier, Bob Lanier, Willis Reed, Randy Smith, David Thompson, Jerry West, and Lenny Wilkens.

10. Bobby Jones of the Philadelphia 76ers has been getting considerable publicity of late, but not necessarily for his scoring or playmaking. Explain.

11. What does Billy Cunningham, the coach of the 76ers, have in common with Bobby Jones?

12. You undoubtedly know that Madison Square Garden is in New York City. But do you know where the following arenas are? The Omni, The Spectrum, The Summit, The HemisFair Arena, McNichols Sports Arena, Reunion Arena, Memorial Coliseum, and Veterans Memorial Coliseum

ANSWERS

1. *Nate "Tiny" Archibald, 6-feet 1-inch. He took the NBA scoring title in 1972–73.*

2. *Kareem Abdul-Jabbar, 7-feet 2-inches.*

3. *Willis Reed of the New York Knicks is the only player in this group to win the MVP award. He was named MVP once, in 1969–70, when the Knicks defeated the Lakers, four games to three, in the NBA championship finals. That was a big year for Reed. He was also named MVP in the All-Star game, which saw the East defeat the West, 142–135.*

4. *Dave DeBusschere. Upon his graduation from the University of Detroit in 1962, DeBusschere signed two pro contracts—one with the Detroit Pistons, and another one with the Chicago White Sox for a reported bonus of $160,000. His baseball career was confined to the minor leagues for the most part, although he did appear in 36 major-league games as a pitcher for the White Sox. He gave up his dual career to concentrate on basketball in 1964, at the age of twenty-four, when the Pistons offered him the job of player-coach. He lasted two years as a coach, winning 79 games and losing 143. Detroit traded him to the Knicks in 1968.*

5. *On November 8, 1978, the Philadelphia 76ers defeated the New Jersey Nets, 137–133. But the Nets later protested that three technical fouls had been called against player Bernard King in violation of league rules that specify that no more than two technicals can be assessed against any one person in the same game. Commissioner Lawrence O'Brien upheld the protest and ruled that the last 17 minutes and 50 seconds of that game be replayed—this was the point at which King's third technical had been called. That part of the game was replayed in March 1979, and once again the 76ers won, this time by a score of 123–117. In* the meantime, three of the players who had appeared in the original game on November 8 had been traded to their opposing teams—two from the 76ers to the Nets, and one from the Nets to the 76ers—and thus played for both teams in the same game.

6. Gus Johnson of the Baltimore Bullets.

7. Tom McMillen, 6-foot 11-inch forward for the Atlanta Hawks.

8. Darryl Dawkins, 6-foot 11-inch center for the 76ers. He went directly from high school in Orlando, Florida, to the 76ers.

9. They were each named MVP of the All-Star games during the 1970s

10. He is the "sixth man" for the Philadelphia 76ers.

11. Billy Cunningham, coach of the 76ers, was the "sixth man" on the 76ers' famous team of 1966–67.

12. The Omni, Atlanta; The Spectrum, Philadelphia; The Summit, Houston; The HemisFair Arena, San Antonio; McNichols Sports Arena, Denver; Reunion Arena, Dallas; Memorial Coliseum, Portland; and Veterans Memorial Coliseum, Phoenix.

FOURTH OVERTIME

Women's Basketball

Women have been playing basketball as long as men, although only in recent years has women's basketball attracted attention as a major sport. From the very beginning, women took to basketball with enthusiasm, but the modified rules under which they played made their game placid and static. Women's rules have only recently approximated men's, and it was not until 1970 that the number of players per side for women was established at five. Prior to that time, women's basketball was played with six players on each side.

In 1926 the Amateur Athletic Union, which had been conducting men's national basketball championships since 1897, staged the first National AAU championship for women, and has conducted annual championships ever since. As with the men, many of the women's teams appearing in these AAU tournaments are sponsored by industrial or commercial businesses. Some of the earlier women's championship teams were sponsored by Sunoco Oil, Tulsa Business College, Vultee Aircraft, Hanes Hosiery Mills, and Nashville Business College.

A significant change occurred in the status of women's basketball in 1972, when Congress passed the Education Amendments Act. Title IX of this act prohibited discrimination on the basis of sex in intercollegiate and scholastic sports. This meant that women's collegiate athletics were to have the same rights and the same budgets as men's athletics. It hasn't quite happened that way as yet, but there has been marked improvement.

As an example, in the 1972–73 season the budget for all

women's athletics at UCLA was $60,000, while that for men's sports was $5 million. (In many other colleges, the total women's budget was only $1,000, not even enough to buy uniforms. The women used T-shirts or gym clothes.) For 1980–81 the budget for women's athletics at UCLA rose to $1.1 million, still far below the millions for men, but certainly far above the $60,000 of a few years before. Similar increases have taken place at other colleges, and women's collegiate basketball games are now getting national television coverage.

Bolstered by Title IX, the Association for Intercollegiate Athletics for Women (AIAW) has been conducting annual tournaments for the top women's intercollegiate teams. And the Women's Pro Basketball League, while still suffering growing pains (it began in 1978–79), looks to be a serious contender for ultimate consideration as a big-league sport.

In a more recent development, the NCAA—the organization governing men's sports—voted to sponsor major women's championship tournaments in nine sports, including basketball, during the 1981–82 season.

With more and more media coverage, ever-increasing collegiate budgets, and a pro league that is determined to succeed, women's basketball has become an integral part of the sports scene. It will unquestionably last as long as the game itself.

1. One of the first intercollegiate women's basketball games was played on April 4, 1896, between the University of California and Stanford University. Stanford defeated California 2–1. But there is another feature of this game that is far more intriguing than the game itself or the final score. Explain.

2. In 1931 one of the most famous of all women athletes made her basketball debut with the Golden Cyclones of Dallas, Texas, and led them to that season's AAU title. Two years later she entered the pro-basketball ranks to play with the Brooklyn Yankees. Name her.

3. In the years since 1926 the AAU women's championships have seen some powerhouse teams, notably Wayland College of Plainview, Texas, which won six titles during the 1950s and 1960s, and Nashville Business College of Tennessee, which won ten titles in the same two decades. The AIAW has its own powerful teams. Name the team that won the first AIAW championship, played in 1972. This same team went on to take the next two titles.

4. Another team took the next three AIAW titles. Name this team.

5. Both of these are small colleges. By 1978, when the Title IX provisions began to make themselves felt, dominance in women's basketball shifted to the larger schools. UCLA won the title in 1978, and it seemed for awhile as if it might well establish a dynasty in women's basketball as its men's teams had done the decade before. But it was not to be. The championships in 1979 and 1980 were taken by a team from Norfolk, Virginia. What school?

6. One of the players on those two championship teams is now in the Women's Basketball League, playing pro basketball as a 6-foot 5-inch center for the Chicago Hustle. Name her.

7. A collegiate teammate of hers, a 5-foot 10-inch, 146-

pound guard, now with the Dallas Diamonds of the WBL, is the most talked-about woman player of the moment. She has not yet established herself as the supreme superstar of the WBL, but her aggressive style and her willingness to "play like a man" mark her as a coming superstar in pro ranks. Who is she?

8. As a junior and senior in college, in 1979 and 1980, she won the most prestigious of all awards in women's collegiate basketball. What award?

9. A 5-foot, 9-inch, 140-pound forward from UCLA named Ann Meyers made headlines in September 1979. Why?

10. Ann Meyers is now starring in the WBL. With what team?

11. A teammate of hers is known to basketball aficionados as "The Blaze." What's her full name?

12. The NBA has "Pistol Pete" Maravich. The WBL has a player with an even more formidable nickname. What player, and what is her nickname?

13. Twins Dick and Tom Van Arsdale played in the NBA. The WBL has its own set of twins, playing for the same team. Name them, and name their team.

14. Which team won the first WBL championship—for the 1978–79 season?

15. Who won the WBL's first MVP award?

16. Who are the American Redheads?

ANSWERS

1. The intercollegiate women's basketball game between California and Stanford had an audience of 700, all women. At California's insistence, no men were allowed to see the game.

2. Mildred "Babe" Didrikson.

3. Immaculata of Philadelphia, Pennsylvania.

4. Delta State of Cleveland, Mississippi.

5. Old Dominion.

6. Inge Nissen.

7. Nancy Lieberman.

8. The Wade Trophy as the best women's collegiate player.

9. On September 12, 1979, the Indiana Pacers of the NBA announced at a press conference in Los Angeles that they had signed Ann Meyers for one year at a reported salary of $50,000. To charges that this was a promotional stunt, pitting her against the much bigger men in the NBA, Ms. Meyers replied: "If I didn't think I could compete, I wouldn't be there. I don't want to embarrass anyone, including myself." She was cut by the Pacers two weeks later.

10. The New Jersey Gems. She signed a three-year contract with them in November 1979 for a reported $130,000.

11. Carol Blazejowski. Her three-year package is reportedly worth $150,000 and bonuses.

12. "Machine Gun" Molly Bohn 5-foot 9-inch guard for the San Francisco Pioneers.

13. *Faye and Kaye Young of the New Jersey Gems.*

14. *The Houston Angels.*

15. *Rita Easterling, 5-foot 6-inch guard for the Chicago Hustle.*

16. *The American Redheads are a women's barnstorming team. They are all 6 feet and over, and all are redheads (or at least they claim to be). They have been barnstorming across the country for many years, and are good enough to beat most men's teams.*

DEE-fense!
DEE-fense!

As in other sports, basketball has developed its own vocabulary. To help you understand and enjoy the game to its fullest, either as a spectator or participant, this final section of our book contains a brief glossary of some of the more commonly used words and phrases in basketball.

air ball—A shot that misses everything, basket and backboard.

assist—A pass from one teammate to another that directly results in a field goal.

backcourt—The half of the court nearer the basket that is being defended. (See frontcourt.)

backcourt player—A guard. Visualize an area that looks like a horseshoe, extending from the corners fifteen to thirty feet from the basket on defense. It is this area that the backcourt player guards. Guards are usually the smallest players on a team, and the fastest. On offense, the guard is the player that generally brings the ball downcourt from his backcourt to his frontcourt.

backdoor play—A play directly under the basket and behind the backs of the defenders. An offensive player sneaks in behind the backs of the defenders and takes a pass from a teammate under the basket for a backdoor play.

bank shot—A shot bounced or caromed off the backboard.

baseline—An end line

blocking—Illegally impeding the progress of an opponent who doesn't have the ball.

bonus shot—An additional free throw.

buzzer—The device that is sounded to signal the end of each period.

buzzer shot—A shot made in an attempt to score as the buzzer sounds.

center—The pivot man, normally the tallest player on the squad. At one time, centers were 6-feet 8-inches, 6-feet 9-inches, and occasionally 6-feet 10-inches. Today, it is not unusual to have centers 7 feet and over. The center has to be big, tough, and aggressive, since he is involved in many plays—blocking shots, rebounding, passing, shooting. He also is the one who makes the jump for the jump ball that starts each period.

charging—An offensive foul committed when the player with the ball runs into a defensive player who has established his position.

clear the boards—To get a rebound.

control the boards—To get *most* of the rebounds.

cornerman—A forward. The forwards, who are usually taller than the guards, but not quite as tall as the center, stay in around the basket and the corners, and generally do not shoot from farther out, as do the guards.

double team—Two defensive players guarding one offensive player.

drive—A move toward the basket by a dribbler in an attempt to score.

dunk—Forcing or pushing the ball through the basket with the hands directly from above after a leap high toward the basket. (See *stuff shot.*)

extra period—An additional or overtime period if the score is tied at the end of regulation play. Basketball games cannot end in a tie.

fast break—Originally a fast break was a maneuver that sent one player, usually the fastest man and the best shooter, downcourt for an easy layup before the other team got set. Today, a fast break tries to involve the entire team, including the rebounder. For a fast break to be effective, enough of the offensive team must move with the ball into its frontcourt faster than the defenders so that an easy percentage shot is possible.

feed—To hand the ball to a teammate or pass it off to him when he is likely to score.

field goal—A shot from the court, good for either two or three points depending upon the distance.

forward—See *cornerman.*

free throw—A penalty shot awarded after a foul.

free throw lane—A lane 19 feet long, which runs from the free throw line where the fouled player stands for his shot, to the baseline and 15 feet from the free throw line to the backboard. In college play, the free throw lane is 12 feet wide; in professional basketball, the lane is 16 feet wide.

freeze the ball—Hanging on to the ball with little or no attempt to score. Done more often in college play, which has no 24-second clock, but can also happen in pro ball when an offensive team has the ball with *less* than 24 seconds to play in a period or in the game.

frontcourt—The half of the court that contains the basket where the offense is trying to score (See *backcourt.*)

guard—See *backcourt player.*

hacking—Striking the player who has the ball across the hands, wrists, or forearms. Hacking is a personal foul called against the defending player.

hand-checking—Permitted in professional basketball only, not in colleges or high schools. A defensive player may keep one hand on an opponent, provided his hand doesn't keep his opponent from moving freely.

held ball—Occurs when two players go for a loose ball at the same time and neither can gain control of it without undue roughness. (See *jump ball.*)

high post—A position near the outer circle of the free-throw line.

jump ball—At the beginning of each period, any two opponents—normally the centers, since they are the tallest—stand in the center circle at midcourt. An official throws the ball up in the air above the two players, who simultaneously jump for the ball and try to tap it to a teammate. A jump ball is also used between two players involved in a held ball, at or near the spot where the held ball occurred.

jumper—A jump shot.

key or *keyhole*—The free-throw lane and the circle at the top. When the free-throw lane was 6 feet wide, it *looked* like a keyhole. With the lane now much wider, it no longer looks like a keyhole, but is still referred to as the key or keyhole.

kill the clock—To stall or freeze the ball long enough to get the last shot in a period.

layup—An easy shot, often taken after the player breaks away from his defenders. According to Knick coach Red Holzman, "A player should come into the hoop at an angle–45 degrees, if that is possible. . . . (The) best way to make a layup is off the backboard." A layup can also be stuffed, or dunked.

lose the handle—To lose control of the ball and turn it over to the other team.

low post—A position at the side of the basket outside of the free-throw lane.

matchup—Matching one player from Team A against his counterpart in Team B.

mismatch—Occurs when a defender suddenly finds himself covering a much larger and taller player because of a defensive switch.

one-and-one—A free throw and a bonus free throw, awarded only if the fouled player makes his first free throw.

one-on-one—A confrontation between a dribbler and one defender, in which the dribbler is using every legal tactic to score, and conversely, the defender is trying to stop him from scoring.

outlet pass—Passing to a teammate along the sideline or downcourt by a player who has just taken a defensive rebound.

over the limit—When a team has committed more than its prescribed limit of fouls, it is over the limit, and the other team is then permitted bonus free throws.

penalty free throw—In professional basketball, the extra free throw awarded to a team when the opposing team is over the limit.

penetration—Moving with the ball through the entire defense directly to the basket. This tricky maneuver requires a fast man, expert dribbling, and the ability to feint out the defenders.

percentage shot—A shot that will be made more often than it is missed. The closer to the basket, the better the percentage. Three-point field goals are not percentage shots.

pivot man—Normally, the center, who will play with his back to the basket on offense, and be ready to pivot into the basket with the ball. The center is also the pivot around which an offense revolves.

play loose—To guard an opponent from a distance.

play tight—To guard an opponent closely.

point guard—The playmaker, the fastest man on the team, the one who directs the attack.

rainbow shot—A high arcing shot, usually from the outside over the heads of tall defenders.

rebound—Occurs after a shot taken at the basket fails to go in. When the ball bounces off the backboard or the rim of the basket, it becomes a free ball and is then called a rebound. The team that takes the rebound has possession of the ball, and either goes on offense or stays on offense.

set shot—An attempted field goal taken by a player who stands with both feet on the floor, well away from the basket.

showboating—Fancy behind-the-back dribbling.

squad—A total of twelve men in pro basketball. Of the five on the floor, one is a center, two are forwards, and two are guards.

stuff shot—Stuffing the ball into the basket from above after a leap high toward the basket. (See *dunk*.)

switch—Occurs when a defending team is using a man-to-man defense. To avoid being blocked out when offensive players crisscross, the defenders call "switch" and automatically change the man they were assigned to guard; each defender will then pick up the player closest to him. (See *mismatch*.)

ten-second violation—Failure to bring the ball across the midcourt within ten seconds after gaining possession of the ball in the backcourt. This violation results in a turnover to the other team.

three-point play—When a player is fouled in the act of shooting, and he makes the basket, he is awarded a free throw. If he makes that as well, it becomes a three-point play. A three-point play is also a three-point field goal.

three-second violation—Occurs when an offensive player remains in the free-throw lane, or keyhole, longer than three seconds while his or her team is in control of the ball. When that happens, the ball is turned over to the other team.

traveling—Walking with the ball, or taking too many steps without dribbling.

twenty-four-second violation—In pro basketball, failure to take a shot within twenty-four seconds after gaining possession of the ball. Again, this violation results in a turnover to the other team.

wipeout—To win by a big margin.

zone defense—Used in college basketball only. To guard a particular area of a zone rather than guarding a specified opposing player, as in man-to-man Offensive players will move about and pass the ball back and forth, but players in a zone defense will stick to their assigned areas. When a zone defense is used, it involves all five defenders, all of whom form a tight horseshoe under the basket and try to keep their opponents from penetrating through the zone to the basket.